TAKE ACTION!

A Guide To Active Citizenship

Craig Kielburger

Marc Kielburger

(Log In)

TAKE ACTION! A Guide To Active Citizenship

HOME
Preface, Contents

PART I
How To Get Involved: The Step-By-Step Process

PART II
The 'How To' Guide

TAKE ACTION! A Guide To Active Citizenship

HOME	PART I	PART II
Preface, Contents	**How To Get Involved:**	**The 'How To' Guide**
	The Step-By-Step Process	

A MESSAGE FROM MARC AND CRAIG

For over a decade now, the young

leaders at Free The Children and Me to We have been passionately engaged in changing the world. As a team of dedicated youth, we've come a long way—but not without help.

Having enjoyed the support of others, we quickly learned that young people are capable of great things, yet they often lack the tools to make a change. This step-by-step guide has been designed to show you how to get organized and get moving to tackle important issues in your community, your school, your country, and around the world. As our mentors did with us, we hope that Take Action! will guide your first steps toward global citizenship. It represents all of our many "lessons learned" and will teach you how to best organize, educate and empower other young people to make a change in the world and become global citizens.

With each new section, you will learn how to break down and tackle even the most difficult social problems; how to channel your passion for a better world into concrete actions—both large and small. You will also begin to develop and hone the skills that will make your actions speak louder, and discover how other young people are taking up the challenge of confronting injustice in creative ways.

Before you begin your journey, here are some words of encouragement. When dealing with tough issues, it is easy to feel powerless and alone. But as an African proverb says, "When spider webs unite, they can tie up a lion." This reminds us that, when we come together as citizens of a global community, we can tackle injustice and secure bright futures for the world's many people. This consciousness and solidarity begins with us, with youth.

Remember, we are the generation that we have been waiting for!

Let's get started.

Marc and Craig

Marc Kielburger
Co-Founder
Free The Children

Craig Kielburger
Founder and Chair
Free The Children

Photo © V. Tony Hauser

TAKE Action! A Guide To Active Citizenship

Home	PART I	PART II
Preface, Contents	How To Get Involved: The Step-By-Step Process	The 'How To' Guide

Seven Steps To Social Involvement

SOUND BYTES: `OK!`

> "The unselfish effort to bring cheer to others will be the beginning of a happier life for ourselves."
>
> *Helen Keller (1880-1968) Author and educator*

Seven Steps to Social Involvement

Are you interested in becoming socially involved?

Have you come across a social issue that motivates you but you are uncertain about where to start to make a difference? You are not alone. It is often very difficult to become socially active. Many of the issues currently facing the world, such as child labor, HIV/AIDS, or war and conflict, are complicated and controversial. However, simply because an issue is difficult does not mean you should avoid becoming involved in it. Frequently, the more complex the issue, the more your help is needed to bring about change. This section of the book introduces you to seven easy steps you can take to break down the issue into manageable stages for your social involvement. Following the suggestions outlined for each step will help you become a more effective social advocate. Try to use these seven steps every time you pick a new issue in which to become active.

Doing so will maximize the impact of your involvement.

STEP 1: CHOOSE AN ISSUE

The first and most important step in becoming socially involved is to choose an issue that you are passionate about. Ask yourself: What social issue motivates and inspires me? Try to find an issue that you would like to research in order to learn as much as you can.

There are so many ways that you can make a difference! What issues are important to you?

Be Observant and Ask Questions

Is there something in the world that does not seem fair or just to you? Perhaps you have read about it in a newspaper or on the Internet, or seen it on television. Is there anything that you would like to change at school, in your community, or in the world?

When choosing your issue, try to be as specific as possible. If your issue is, for example, "war and conflict," try to focus on one particular aspect of that issue. You could become involved in ridding the world of nuclear weapons or addressing the issue of child soldiers in war-torn countries. The following chart lists other examples:

PART III
Where You Can Get Involved-
Everywhere!

PART IV
Tackling Social Issues

PART V
Sources And Resources,
End Notes

ISSUE	SPECIFIC PROBLEM
Human Rights	Women in the world are not treated equally to men when it comes to receiving an education.
Children's Rights	A local store is importing clothes made in sweatshops that employ children.
The Environment	Over-fishing is threatening many marine species with extinction.
Hunger	Students at my school are hungry; children in many developing countries are starving.
Poverty	Our city lacks shelters for the thousands of homeless people.
HIV/AIDS	Millions of men, women and children in sub-Saharan Africa are dying of AIDS.
Peace	Many war criminals are never brought to justice.

Once you have chosen your issue, find out what other organized groups are already addressing this issue, or associated issues. Thoroughly research the groups to make sure they are legitimate and credible, and then consider approaching them for help with tackling your issue. You may also want to research to determine how other individuals and groups are making significant contributions in your community.

SOUND BYTES: OK!

"You gain strength, courage, and confidence by every experience in which you really stop to look fear in the face."

Eleanor Roosevelt (1884-1962) Author and human rights activist

STEP 2: DO YOUR RESEARCH

It is important to learn more about the problems that prevent millions of people around the world from being healthy, happy, and reaching their full potential. If you want to make a difference in their lives, you have to educate yourself. You have to know what you are fighting for.

Read newspapers and magazines to keep up-to-date on current events. Then visit the library to learn more about the topics that sparked your interest. If an issue is too large to learn about all at once, remember to break it down into several smaller issues and think about the different aspects of each problem. This will make your research more manageable.

Begin by determining what specific issues are related to your topic. For example:

PART III
Where You Can Get Involved-
Everywhere!

PART IV
Tackling Social Issues

PART V
Sources And Resources,
End Notes

POVERTY >

**ISSUES RELATED
TO POVERTY >**

Unemployment

Illiteracy

Child labor

Homelessness

Disease

Social isolation

Where can you obtain information?

- Library
- Textbooks
- Internet
- Teachers, principal, parents/guardians, and community leaders
- News media
- Government
- Surveys and interviews
- Organizations and community groups
- Corporations and local businesses
- Magazines and newspapers
- Films

Begin your research by making a list of specific questions concerning the issue, and then set out to answer them. To gain a broader understanding of the problem you are researching, think about its causes, its consequences, and its possible solutions.

TAKE ACTION! A Guide To Active Citizenship

HOME Preface, Contents	PART I How To Get Involved: The Step-By-Step Process	PART II The 'How To' Guide

Example Issue: Child Labor

Here are some questions you might ask yourself:

Causes
- What is child labor?
- Why are children working? What situations force children into child labor?
- Where are they working? In which countries is child labor extensive? What kinds of industries employ children?

Consequences
- How many children are working?
- What kind of work do they do? What are the dangers involved in child labor?
- Is all work harmful to children? Are there any advantages to child labor?
- Who is benefiting from child labor?
- What are the long-term costs of the problem if no change takes place?

Solutions
- What is being done to solve the problem? What does and does not work?
- Who are the decision-makers I need to approach in order to solve the problem?
- What laws are in effect in various countries to protect children? Are additional laws needed?
- What can I do to make a difference?

Researching Made Easy

Tip 1: Choose a Direction
Before you dive into your research, consider what the information will be used for: a fundraising campaign, a speech, a report, an information display, a flyer or pamphlet. This will give you an idea of the kind of material you are looking for, as well as how much research information you will need for your project.

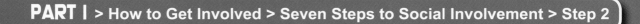

PART III
Where You Can Get Involved-
Everywhere!

PART IV
Tackling Social Issues

PART V
Sources And Resources,
End Notes

Tip 2: Set a Goal and a Deadline

Set a goal for each study session. Know what you want to accomplish and give yourself a deadline. For example, tell yourself that you will read and take notes on three one-page newspaper articles in one hour.

Try to set a reasonable goal, one that you will be able to reach if you work hard. That way, you will finish your study session feeling good about yourself and the work you have done.

Tip 3: Tackle One Thing at a Time

In your reading, you might come across other topics that spark your interest. Do some investigating, explore, and then make a note to return to it later to dig deeper, but try to stay focused on the task at hand. It is easier to concentrate and more will be accomplished if you focus on only a few things at one time.

Tip 4: Organize Your Information

As you conduct research, you will need to organize the information you obtain. You may wish to use such methods as summaries, notes, timelines, visual organizers, maps, or comparison organizers. Make sure that the method you choose suits the information you are trying to organize, and remember to accurately document your sources of information.

Tip 5: Get Others Involved

Is there too much to do? If so, make the research task a group project. Research is a great way to get others interested and involved in your cause. Divide up your issue into different subjects and have each group member take ownership of one of the subjects. After some initial research, share what you have learned with the group. This way, you will all gain a more complete understanding of the issue.

Tip 6: Ask the Experts

Contact organizations that are devoted to the issue you are researching. They can direct you to reliable resources and provide you with some information to get started. (See Part 5 for contact information that may help you.)

How to Be a Critical Reader

Do not believe everything you read

When doing research, it is important to compare different sources before you accept as true what one book says. Do not be impressed by words just because they are in print. Be critical of information. Books are not always accurate; sometimes their statistics are outdated or incorrect. The numbers you find might either be reduced or exaggerated, depending on how the writer wants you to react. If you have information from a variety of sources, you can compare it and see if the sources agree and their numbers match up. And if they do not, then you have some more investigating to do.

Beware of bias

Whether or not they are conscious of it, every writer has a different point of view, also known as *bias*. The way they grew up and the experiences they have had have shaped their perception and interpretation of the world around them. In order to determine the bias contained in the material you are reading, consider the following:

PART III Where You Can Get Involved-Everywhere!	**PART IV** Tackling Social Issues	**PART V** Sources And Resources, End Notes

- Author: Who is the author? What kind of education or experience has this person had? Is he or she an expert on the subject? From what political, social, and economic position is this author writing?
- Audience: What audience was the article intended for?
- Intent: Why was this article written? What main point is the author trying to convince you of?

Consider both sides of the issue

Once you start reading, chances are you will uncover many interesting facts, but some might surprise or shock you. So before you get carried away, make sure you have the whole story. Researching a topic means looking at both sides of the issue. This is the only way to get a clear, unbiased understanding of what is really going on. It is important to consider both the positive and the negative aspects of the issue before forming an opinion. Doing so will help you to devise more effective solutions and will make your argument stronger when you are ready to take a stand.

Documentation: Know your source

Because you are young, some people will challenge your facts. If this happens, demonstrate that you have done your homework!

As you research, write down all the bibliographical information about your sources. Check the references cited or the bibliography of your source to find out where the author obtained his or her information. Make sure that your information is coming from an informed and reliable source and that your notes are accurate.

If you can support your statements with solid facts, you will be confident in sharing what you have learned.

The Internet as a Research Tool

The Internet puts an unlimited amount of information at your fingertips, but how reliable is it all? The fact is that anyone can have a site on the Internet. There are often no editors and no supervisors, no one to make sure that what is floating around in cyberspace is true. The trick to doing research on the Internet is to learn to distinguish between fact and opinion, and to confirm the information you find. Think of the Internet as one resource, not the only resource.

TAKE ACTION! A Guide To Active Citizenship

Home	PART I	PART II
Preface, Contents	How To Get Involved: The Step-By-Step Process	The 'How To' Guide

What Can You Rely On?

Generally speaking, you can assume that the information contained on a website set up by a university, government, or major institution is reliable. Because they have a reputation to uphold, these sources usually make sure that the information they post is accurate. But keep in mind that every organization has its own agenda, so it is always best to check more than one source when you are doing your research.

PART III
Where You Can Get Involved-
Everywhere!

PART IV
Tackling Social Issues

PART V
Sources And Resources,
End Notes

A Checklist for the Wise Web Researcher

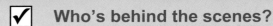

✓ **Who's behind the scenes?**
- Are the authors of the site identified?
- What qualifications do they have?
- What kind of professional or institutional associations do the authors have?
- Is there an e-mail address that you can use to contact the authors and ask questions?
- Are there links to reliable sites where the accuracy of the information can be confirmed?

✓ **Is the site up-to-date?**
- Is there a date when the site was last updated?
- If so, has the information been revised recently?

✓ **Documentation and accuracy**
- Are there references or a bibliography to verify that the information is true?
- Does the site credit the sources of its information? (A reliable source states clearly where the information originated from.)
- Based on the research you have already done, does the information on the site seem accurate?

✓ **Intention**
- What is the goal of the site? What is it trying to convince you of?
- Can you sense a bias in the visual or written material?
- Is a stereotype being promoted?

✓ **Language**
- Is the language professional and appropriate?
- Does the site use proper grammar, spelling, and punctuation?

TAKE ACTION! A Guide To Active Citizenship

| **Home** Preface, Contents | **PART I** How To Get Involved: The Step-By-Step Process | **PART II** The 'How To' Guide |

STEP 3: BUILD A TEAM

Tell others about your issue, and ask them if they want to help. When people see that you are sincere about your area of concern, and hear you explain why it is important to help, some of them will want to get involved. These people will be your teammates and you will grow to rely on their support, advice, and ideas. Remember, any successful team respects the rights and opinions of all its members.

SOUND BYTES: OK!

⚠️ "There is no 'I' in teamwork!"

Anonymous

How to Get Others Involved

Concerned that no one will want to join your team and become involved in a social issue that needs change? Here are some strategies for motivating others to become active and socially committed:

PART III
Where You Can Get Involved-
Everywhere!

PART IV
Tackling Social Issues

PART V
Sources And Resources,
End Notes

Talk to...

- your family and friends
- people in your school and community
- your teachers and principal

Seek permission to hold an information presentation...

- for students in your class and school
- at your local church, synagogue, temple, mosque, or other place of worship
- at community gatherings
- at sports clubs in which you are involved

TAKE ACTION! A Guide To Active Citizenship

| **Home** Preface, Contents | **PART I** How To Get Involved: The Step-By-Step Process | **PART II** The 'How To' Guide |

Promote the issue by...
- hosting a party
- putting on a play
- organizing an exhibit
- hosting a sporting event
- distributing flyers at school or in the community

Exercise strong team leadership by...
- understanding and celebrating differences among team members
- welcoming everyone's contribution
- utilizing individual talents
- building a team representative of various cultures and communities
- identifying what else can be done to get others involved

SOUND BYTES:

OK

"If you risk nothing, then you risk everything."

Geena Davis (b. 1957) Actor

STEP 4: CALL THE MEETING

Once you have a group of people who are interested in your cause, it is time to call a formal meeting. (See Part 3 for more information on how to hold a meeting.)

You may find that holding your first meeting is among the most difficult steps, but take heart. Organizing effective and efficient meetings takes a lot of practice. Here are some points to keep in mind when you organize your first meeting:

PART III
Where You Can Get Involved-
Everywhere!

PART IV
Tackling Social Issues

PART V
Sources And Resources,
End Notes

Find a Place to Hold the Meeting

Where will your meeting be held? Will you need to seek permission to hold the meeting? Some possible meeting places include:

- home
- school
- hall or place of worship
- community center
- local library
- restaurant

Set an Agenda for the Meeting

- Have a definite purpose in mind for the meeting.
- Outline the points to be discussed.
- Prepare written material/information for presentation to the group.(See Part 2 for more information on agendas.)

Conduct the Meeting

- Thank everyone for coming.
- Outline the purpose of the meeting.
- Have someone take notes or record on audiotape what is said.
- Discuss what you have learned from your research.
- Make a plan of action with the group.

Conclude the Meeting

- Set a date for a second meeting.
- Establish where the next meeting will be held.
- Discuss the purpose of the next meeting.
- Ask for help with organizing the next meeting.

Tip!

At the meeting, it is crucial that all of your teammates understand the issue. Members of the team can also research and share what they have discovered with others at the meeting. This will help everyone understand the issue more fully.

TAKE ACTION! A Guide To Active Citizenship

| **Home** Preface, Contents | **PART I** How To Get Involved: The Step-By-Step Process | **PART II** The 'How To' Guide |

STEP 5: MAKE A PLAN OF ACTION

Making a plan of action is often one of the most exciting steps. Your action plan will be your guide and compass in making a difference in your social issue. How do you make a plan of action? By brainstorming! Come up with creative, crazy, and fun ideas and ways to take positive action on your issue.

Here are a few brainstorming tips:
- Identify a recorder to write down all the ideas.
- Allow enough time for every team member to talk.
- Listen attentively.
- Be positive. Everyone's ideas have value.
- Be creative. All ideas have potential.

In your first brainstorming session, you may want to do the following:

1. Define your goal: What does your group hope to accomplish?

It is helpful for the group to have a mandate. A mandate is a statement that describes the purpose of the group. Here are two examples of mandates for groups of young people who are concerned about child poverty:

"Our mandate is to hold a food drive to collect food for the local food bank so poor kids in our community will not have to be hungry."

"Our mandate is to get the school board to provide a breakfast program to needy students in all the schools in our district so no kid has to go to class hungry."

2. List the names of those people who will be helpful and those who might oppose your action.
- Who has the power and the authority to make the changes you want?
- How can adults help?
- Who will oppose your idea? Why?
- How will you address opposition?

PART III
Where You Can Get Involved-
Everywhere!

PART IV
Tackling Social Issues

PART V
Sources And Resources,
End Notes

3. Develop a strategy

- How much time can the members give to the cause?
- What responsibility will each person have?
- What role will adults play? (Although adults can play an important role, do not let adults take over your group. Remember, you are a youth organization.)

4. Create a message or logo for your cause

- Develop a youth friendly and fun logo with lots of color. For example, the Free The Children logo depicts an artistic interpretation of people linking arms around the world. It is simple, fun, distinctive, and colorful.
- Think of the messages and sayings that you want people to remember about your issue and your group. For example, Free The Children uses the message, "children helping children through education."

Free The Children
children helping children through education

5. Map out actions on a calendar

- Make sure that you give yourself enough time to plan each action thoroughly.
- Take time for some fun.
- Evaluate your actions regularly.
- How often can the team meet? Where?

TAKE ACtioN! A Guide To Active Citizenship

| **Home** Preface, Contents | **PART I** How To Get Involved: The Step-By-Step Process | **PART II** The 'How To' Guide |

6. Media and education

- How will you create greater awareness of the issue?
- How will you use the media to help?
- How will you advertise what you are doing?

7. Create a budget

- How much money will you need to carry out your plan? You might need to pay for postage or buy supplies. What else will you need?
- How can money be raised?
- How will transportation be arranged?
- Which companies, organizations, or groups can be approached for donations?

PART III
Where You Can Get Involved-
Everywhere!

PART IV
Tackling Social Issues

PART V
Sources And Resources,
End Notes

STEP 6:
TAKE ACTION AND THEN REVIEW

Taking action is key to turning your ideas into reality. If you are organizing a human rights awareness day, make certain you follow through on your idea. If you are collecting food for your local food bank, do your very best to collect as many kits as you can. It is actions that create real and lasting change in the world.

Once you have acted, it is important to review and evaluate each action so that you can become more effective. You may want to look at the planning, the actions taken, the media, the people involved, and the results. Here are some questions you may want to ask yourself:

- What were the positive aspects of the project?
- What were the negative aspects of the project?
- How can we improve our project or actions next time?
- How well did we work as a team?
- What new areas of responsibility do we need to add to our team next time?
- How can we be more effective as a team next time?
- Did the team members encounter any major obstacles?
- What did the team do well to overcome these obstacles?
- Were there any major disagreements? If so, did the team work well to settle the disagreements? If not, what steps need to be taken in the future to solve conflicts?
- Did the team have enough volunteers,money, equipment, and resources? If not, what can the team do next time to meet our project needs?
- Did the team have enough or too much adult guidance and support?
- What did each of us learn or gain from this project?
- What might each of us do differently next time?

TAKE ACTION! A Guide To Active Citizenship

| **HOME** Preface, Contents | **PART I** How To Get Involved: The Step-By-Step Process | **PART II** The 'How To' Guide |

Tip!

Write down your answers to the questions and keep them in a file so that they can be reviewed when you start the next project. Although you may find it difficult to criticize your work, constructive criticism can be very valuable. Be proud of your achievements. Enjoy one another's company and try to think of ways to do even better next time.

STEP 7: HAVE FUN!

Stay motivated. At times, you may feel overwhelmed and may even run into some opposition. When this happens, try to remember why you got involved in the first place. Your goal is to help others make a difference.

Once you have finished your campaign or event, throw a pizza party or go to a movie with your team. Also, do not be afraid of having fun while you are organizing your activities. Try not to lose focus of the task at hand, but do not forget to make your social involvement an enjoyable and memorable experience.

As teammates, inspire and encourage one another. Everyone needs the support and friendship of those who share the same vision and goals. Friends are one of the gifts you give yourself when you get involved in a cause.

PART III
Where You Can Get Involved-
Everywhere!

PART IV
Tackling Social Issues

PART V
Sources And Resources,
End Notes

SOME THOUGHTS TO KEEP YOU GOING

Look at a problem as an opportunity to be creative.

Experiment with new ways of addressing the problem. Try the untried.

- Be willing to change, to rotate responsibilities within your group, and to find other solutions. Seize every opportunity to learn.
- Look at the big picture. Do not let small obstacles or problems get you down.
- Do not forget the purpose of what you are doing. Your belief in the cause will keep you motivated.
- Work with friends. Seek their support. We all need other people.
- Be optimistic. Focus on the good in others, the good in yourself, and the good you are doing, whether your successes are large or small.

SOUND BYTES: OK!

"There is one thing stronger than all the armies in the world, and that is an idea whose time has come."

Victor Hugo (1802-1885) Author, Les Misérables

TAKE ACTiON! A Guide To Active Citizenship

| **Home** Preface, Contents | **PART I** How To Get Involved: The Step-By-Step Process | **PART II** The 'How To' Guide |

HOW TO USE THE TELEPHONE

Most of you are probably experts when it comes to everyday use of the telephone. You already know that the phone is a great way to get in touch with friends, family, or even your favorite pizza delivery place. But what you may not know is that the phone can also be a valuable tool for social action. You can use the phone to organize a meeting or event, interview people, conduct opinion polls, or talk to government officials about your concerns. Here are a few ways to make your phone call a success:

Prepare for Your Call

1. Get permission to use phones at your home or school. Never make long-distance calls without asking.
2. Be organized. Sometimes calling important officials can make you nervous. Before you pick up the phone, prepare a call sheet with the following information and keep it in front of you while you are speaking with your contact. Being prepared will give you confidence.
    - the name of your contact
    - the reason for your call/what you want to ask the person
    - your address and telephone number to give to your contact at the end of the call
3. Make sure you have enough space on your call sheet (or have extra paper nearby) to record any information your contact gives you.

PART III
Where You Can Get Involved-
Everywhere!

PART IV
Tackling Social Issues

PART V
Sources And Resources,
End Notes

Make the Call

4.   Before placing the call, make sure there is no noise around you.

5.   When someone answers the phone, speak clearly and tell the person your name and school or organization.

6.   If you do not have a contact name, briefly state what kind of information you are looking for and ask to be put in touch with the appropriate individual or department.

7.   If your contact is not there, find out when he or she will be available and make yourself a note to call back at that time. You can also leave your name and contact information, a time when you can be reached, and the reason for your call.

8.   Do not give up if your contact does not call back right away. Keep calling until you get the information you need, but always make sure to be calm and polite.

PART II > The How To Guide > How To Use The Telephone

| **PART III** Where You Can Get Involved- Everywhere! | **PART IV** Tackling Social Issues | **PART V** Sources And Resources, End Notes |

When you Reach Your Contact

9.   When you do speak with your contact, tell him or her your name and your school or organization, and then explain why you have called.

10. Write down your contact's response. If you miss something, do not be afraid to ask for clarification.

11.Get the correct name, title, address, and phone extension of your contact and make sure he or she knows how to get in touch with you, too. When spelling your name, use a word to clarify every letter; for example, "L as in 'lemon,' A as in 'apple,'" and so on.

12. After the phone call, review your notes and add anything else that you can remember from the conversation.

Finding Phone Numbers

Phone books are a useful tool for locating individuals, organizations, businesses, and government institutions. Most directories have three sections: white, yellow, and blue. The Yellow Pages™ sometimes appear as part of the directory and sometimes as a separate publication.

The white pages list, in alphabetical order, the phone number(s) of people as well as companies and organizations. To find a number in the white pages, look up the last name of the person or the first name of the company or organization.

The Yellow Pages™ list, in alphabetical order by product or service category, the phone number(s) of businesses, organizations, and professionals. For example, look up pizza and you will find companies that sell pizza; look up physicians and you will find a list of medical professionals, arranged alphabetically by last name and sometimes listing their specialty (for example, "L as in 'lemon,' A as in 'apple,'" and so on).

The blue pages contain government phone numbers. Federal, provincial or state, and municipal or county governments each have their own section. To use the blue pages, you must first know which level of government you need. For example, if you are focusing on garbage pick-up, you must speak to someone in the local government. If you want to speak with one of your national elected officials about global warming, you must look in the national or federal government section.

TAKE ACTION! A Guide To Active Citizenship

| **Home**
Preface, Contents | **PART I**
How To Get Involved:
The Step-By-Step Process | **PART II**
The 'How To' Guide |

Tip!

You can also dial 411 and have the operator do the search for you, but you must know the location and the full name of the person or organization you are calling. There is a fee associated with this service.

There are many websites that provide on-line phone books. Search the web to find one that has a listing for your area. This should be a free service.

Setting up a Calling Tree

An easy way to let many people know about meetings, actions, and planned events is by setting up a calling tree. Be sure to give each caller a complete list of all people on the calling tree. That way, if one caller needs help, another can assist without difficulty. Review and update your list regularly. If any caller proves to be unreliable, substitute his or her name for another:

PART III
Where You Can Get Involved-
Everywhere!

PART IV
Tackling Social Issues

PART V
Sources And Resources,
End Notes

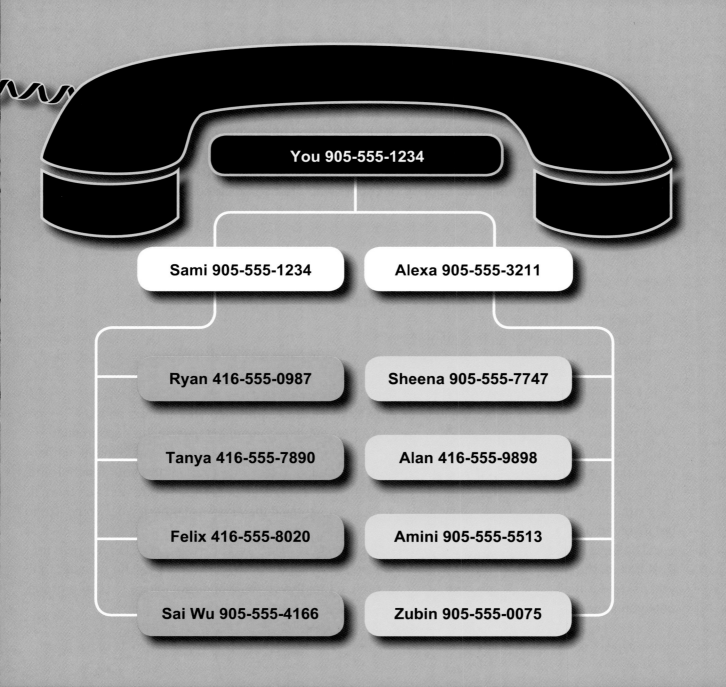

You 905-555-1234

Sami 905-555-1234

Alexa 905-555-3211

Ryan 416-555-0987

Sheena 905-555-7747

Tanya 416-555-7890

Alan 416-555-9898

Felix 416-555-8020

Amini 905-555-5513

Sai Wu 905-555-4166

Zubin 905-555-0075

HOW TO SET UP A GROUP

The first thing to learn about social action is that you cannot take on the world by yourself. No matter how much easier it may sometimes seem to do everything on your own, if you share the work, you will be sure to accomplish more. You will also be giving others the opportunity to get involved in social issues and to realize their potential to be leaders and activists.

The most important skill you will need for the future is teamwork. You will move faster toward your goal if you have the help and support of people who are as dedicated to your cause as you are.

Building Your Core Group

Step 1: Look for Teammates
- Who else is committed to solving this problem?
- Where can you find them?
- What kind of work needs to be done?
- What specific skills might others have to offer?

Step 2: Network
To gather a core group of people dedicated to your cause, start with your friends and classmates. You might want to start by making a presentation to your class (see the section titled "Public Speaking," beginning on page 59), or by talking to people individually. Or, you might simply put up posters in your school to announce the first meeting. (First, however, inform your teacher and your principal of your intention.) Tell them about the issue you are concerned about, and ask them if they would like to help you take action. Ask people you know if they know of others who would like to get involved and if they can introduce you to them.

The keys to gathering support for your cause are networking and perseverance. Do not give up if, at first, some people turn you down. You will be surprised at how many others will be pleased that you asked for their help. Some people do not realize that they have wonderful things to offer a group until you let them know that they are needed.

PART III
Where You Can Get Involved-
Everywhere!

PART IV
Tackling Social Issues

PART V
Sources And Resources,
End Notes

When recruiting, all existing team members should work to make new members feel welcome. Introduce everyone and inform new members of what the group has been doing.

Tip!
If people tell you they are interested in helping, keep all their names, e-mail addresses, and phone numbers on a list so you can contact them to make sure they know about meetings.

Step 3: Build on Your Differences

If you think that everyone in your group has to be the same in order to work well together, think again. An effective group needs a variety of ingredients. When building your team, bring together people with different strengths, talents, perspectives, and experiences. Each person can make a valuable contribution and can help shed new light on old perspectives. It is also a good idea to have some younger and some older members in your group. This ensures the group will continue on year after year even though members change.

The Ingredients for a Great Group

People who are…	Can…
☑ Creative	...think up clever fundraisers
☐ Organized	...plan events and keep the group focused
☐ Artistic	...create posters and information displays
☐ Good writers	...help group members write speeches or letters
☐ Logical	...solve problems
☐ Good communicators	...network with others
☐ Good at math	...take care of finances
☐ Enthusiastic	...motivate the group

TAKE ACTION! A Guide To Active Citizenship

HOME	PART I	PART II
Preface, Contents	How To Get Involved: The Step-By-Step Process	The 'How To' Guide

PART II > The How To Guide > How To Set Up A Group

| **PART III** Where You Can Get Involved-Everywhere! | **PART IV** Tackling Social Issues | **PART V** Sources And Resources, End Notes |

Bringing Out the Best in Your Group

- Find out what skills each person has, and how he or she would be most interested in helping.
- Ask individual members to take the lead in an area where they feel most useful.
- Make sure that everyone is enthusiastic about the role they will play.
- Create a list of rules concerning conduct that you all agree upon. These rules might include respecting each member's opinion and acknowledging each person's right to speak. You might also decide that no one other than the moderator has the right to interrupt others when speaking.
- Use kind words with one another. You are all part of the same team.
- Share and celebrate small victories.

Tip!

The key to building a strong group is inclusion. Do not leave anyone out just because he or she is different. Celebrating your differences will make you powerful. Your opposition will be impressed when they see all kinds of people supporting the same cause.

Step 4: Keep Building

Reach out to new participants even after your core group is established. Their fresh ideas and new perspectives will revitalize your projects and remind you of why you got involved in the first place. Expand your group by making a list of volunteers who may not be able to dedicate themselves completely to your cause, but would like to help out when they have time. Ask your volunteers what their special strengths are and how they would be interested in contributing.

Working in groups can be challenging, but the rewards can be great. Remember the TEAM acronym: Together Everyone Achieves More. By working as a team, you will make new friends and will be able to encourage and support one another. You will also be able to accomplish a great deal more.

TAKe ACTiON! A Guide To Active Citizenship

HOME	PART I	PART II
Preface, Contents	How To Get Involved: The Step-By-Step Process	The 'How To' Guide

SOUND BYTES: OK!

"Teamwork divides the tasks and doubles the success!"

Anonymous

HOW TO HOLD A MEETING

Holding a meeting and providing an opportunity for your team members to share their opinions and ideas can be a powerful force for progress and change. When creative, energetic, and resourceful people come together, anything is possible. However, facilitating an effective meeting can often be tough. It is the leader's job to ensure the opinions of everyone are heard and respected. But he or she must also make certain that the meeting remains productive and on track. The following section will give you some helpful hints on how to hold a successful meeting.

Tip!
The best way to attract people to your meetings is to speak to them in person and invite them to come. People are much more likely to attend a meeting if they have been personally asked or if they have been given a unique role to play.

Step 1: Call a Group Meeting
Arrange a date, time, and location for your first meeting. Once you have a list of people who want to be involved, tell them about the meeting. You may want to hold a meeting at your home, at school, or at a community center. Here are some other details you should address:

PART III
Where You Can Get Involved-
Everywhere!

PART IV
Tackling Social Issues

PART V
Sources And Resources,
End Notes

- Select a location that is convenient, accessible, and large enough to accommodate your group. If necessary, obtain permission from an adult, teacher, or parent/guardian to host your meeting at the location you have selected.
- Set a convenient time for the meeting.
- Remind people about the meeting the day before it is held.

Step 2: Hold a First Meeting

Your first meeting should be simple and short, and viewed as an opportunity for group members to get to know one another. Here are some suggestions for conducting an effective first meeting:

- Thank everyone for coming.
- Take turns making simple introductions or, if possible, find a quick and fun way to 'break the ice' so people feel relaxed and welcome. If there are people in the room who do not yet know one another, this step is particularly important.
- Briefly discuss the issue. Address such questions as: Why are we having this meeting? What are we trying to achieve? How can everyone become involved?
- Value each person's input and encourage questions. Make sure that each person has a chance to speak.
- Set a firm date, time, and location for the second meeting, during which many important decisions will be made.

TAKe Action! A Guide To Active Citizenship

| **Home** Preface, Contents | **PART I** How To Get Involved: The Step-By-Step Process | **PART II** The 'How To' Guide |

Step 3: Hold a Second Meeting

This meeting is key, because it often serves as the basis for your organization or group. Make sure everyone gets involved and participates, and try to accomplish some of the following goals:

- Educate group members about the issue and encourage them to continuously educate themselves on the topic.
- Choose a name for your organization.
- Assign a person to design a number of possible logos and develop potential slogans for your group.
- Brainstorm what type of action your group will take to affect positive change in your chosen social issue. (See "Make a Plan of Action" beginning on page 17 in Part 1 for helpful suggestions.)
- Set goals and a timeline that will help you achieve the actions that you plan to take in working on your social issue of choice.
- Consider assigning responsibilities instead of titles. Some possible roles include the following:
  -organizer of the meeting
  -organizer of events
  -organizer of publicity
  -head of recruitment for new members
  -group recorder (the person in charge of taking notes at meetings)
  -administrator of finances

How to Hold Great Meetings

- Always have an agenda for your meeting.
- Try to attract people who show a real interest in your cause.
- Hold your meetings on regular dates and times; for example, every Friday at 3:00 p.m. in Room 212.
- Set goals for each meeting and achieve them. You may want to ask: Why are we having this meeting and what do we want to accomplish?
- Always keep your team members updated. You can achieve this by phone if your group is small, or by e-mail if your group is large. You may also want to use a bulletin board at school or at your community center.

PART II > The How To Guide > How To Hold A Meeting

| **PART III**
Where You Can Get Involved-
Everywhere! | **PART IV**
Tackling Social Issues | **PART V**
Sources And Resources,
End Notes |

Create an Agenda

An agenda simply outlines the issues that need to be discussed and decided upon by the group. An agenda helps to ensure that everyone stays focused during your meeting and that everything up for discussion is covered before the meeting is over. Here is a sample agenda of a meeting:

Agenda for Teens Taking Action Meeting

Date: October 21, 20—
Location: Meeting to be held in Room 212 at 3:45 p.m.
Time: 3:45: Meeting to be called to order. Issues to be discussed are as follows:

- Introductions. Welcoming of new members to the group.
- Review of decisions made at the last meeting on October 14.
- Announcements and updates since last meeting.
- Planning the next fundraiser for the group. Teens Taking Action needs to decide:
    o What type of fundraiser it will be
    o The date
    o Who will be in charge
    o The next steps that will ensure the fundraiser is a success (making a plan of action)
- Discussion of new business.
- Confirmation of the date and time of next meeting.
- Adjournment of meeting.
- Pizza dinner at Zack's Pizzeria for those who are interested.

During the Meeting

- Start on time.
- Follow your agenda.
- Make certain the meeting has a leader. Meeting leaders are often referred to as moderators. It is the moderator's responsibility to ensure group members participate, are allowed the opportunity to express themselves, and speak in turn. Ideally, take turns assuming the role of moderator so that everyone on the team can learn how to lead meetings.
- Supply materials necessary for the meeting, such as pens, paper, display boards, and so on.
- Arrange seating for the meeting that will promote discussion (for example, sit in a circle).
- Encourage participation.
- Avoid getting into too much detail. Less significant items can be addressed in separate meetings.
- Try to stay on topic. The moderator can make suggestions to keep the group focused.
- As a group, set tasks for people to do for the next meeting.

After the Meeting

- Call or e-mail members who missed the meeting to update them on what they missed.
- Call or e-mail first-time participants and thank them for coming.
- Remind people in advance of tasks they agreed to complete before the next meeting.
- Distribute to all group members a copy of the notes, also called minutes, taken during the meeting so that everyone knows what was discussed and decided upon. Alternatively, e-mail the notes to group members.

Tip!

Invite guest speakers to your meetings occasionally. People who know a lot about your cause can be informative and interesting. They might also share mistakes that their group made when starting out, so that you can try to avoid making those same mistakes.

PART II > The How To Guide > How To Hold A Meeting

| **PART III** Where You Can Get Involved- Everywhere! | **PART IV** Tackling Social Issues | **PART V** Sources And Resources, End Notes |

How to Make Decisions

 Making decisions can be one of the most difficult things your group does.
Here are some hints to help you make good decisions:

- Try to decide on a method of decision-making that everyone agrees with. This step may be challenging, but it is necessary. Some groups like to make decisions by majority vote (when a vote is taken by the members of your organization and the position that is most supported is the decision that is followed); others by general agreement, or consensus.
- Consensus is often the best method of decision-making. It encourages people to work to find solutions and guarantees everyone's opinion is respected.
- If you choose to make decisions by majority vote, determine in advance who among the group is eligible to vote. Is it members of the organization or simply people who attend the meetings? Establishing voting eligibility requirements before a disagreement occurs is preferable. Count everyone's vote equally; no person's vote should be worth more than any other.

- There may be times when team members either have difficulty making up their minds about an issue, or simply disagree. If this occurs, have the moderator list the pros and cons on a chalkboard or piece of chart paper so that everyone can review both sides of the issue and a clear decision can be made.
- Encourage your moderator to consult various books on running a successful meeting. A librarian will be able to help him or her locate suitable resources.

SOUND BYTES: OK!

"The only way you can truly control how you are seen is by being honest all the time."

Tom Hanks (b. 1956) Actor and director

WRITING LETTERS

Writing letters is a good way to tell people what you think, to ask for information, or to work with people in government or organizations. This section will help you write effective letters. You will find helpful examples of several letters written by young people, including:

- a letter to request information
- a thank-you letter
- a letter to a politician
- a letter to the editor of a newspaper or magazine

PART III
Where You Can Get Involved-
Everywhere!

PART IV
Tackling Social Issues

PART V
Sources And Resources,
End Notes

When writing any letter, keep the following hints in mind:
- Type or neatly write your letter. It may look better if it is double-spaced.
- Include the date, your complete return address, phone number, and e-mail address (if applicable) so that you can be contacted.
- Have someone reliable check your letter for spelling mistakes and grammatical errors.

Letter to Request Information

Writing a letter to request information is an easy way to gather materials for your research. Many organizations have information kits for that purpose. When writing a letter to request information, follow these guidelines:
- Try to follow the layout in the sample letter as closely as possible (see page 41). It is a style of letter that is considered professional and is used often in business circles.
- Be as specific as possible in your request, especially when you are asking for government information. Governments have thousands of publications on hundreds of issues. If you are precise and clear when you describe what type of information you need, you are more likely to get the most useful information possible.
- Ask the organization to send you an information package for young people, if they have one.

Tip!

If the organization from which you are requesting information says that there is a cost for the materials, tell them that you are a student, briefly explain your group's mandate, and then ask if they would be willing to donate the materials or provide them at a reduced cost.

Format of a Letter Requesting Information

Your Name
Your full address
Your telephone, fax,
and e-mail information

Date the letter

Name of organization
Person to whom you are writing
Full address

Dear Sir or Madam,

- Identify yourself (state your name, grade, and school).
- Briefly describe your group.
- State your purpose for writing.
- Thank the person to whom you are writing for his or her time.
- Let the person know that you look forward to hearing from him or her.

Sincerely,

Sign your name

Type or print your name

PART III
Where You Can Get Involved-
Everywhere!

PART IV
Tackling Social Issues

PART V
Sources And Resources,
End Notes

Sample Letter Requesting Information

Ari Khan
6888 14th Avenue East
Vancouver, BC
Canada V5P 1R3
Tel: 604-555-0202
Fax: 604-555-1314

November 24, 20—

Children for the Environment
16 Balsam Road
Sudbury, ON
Canada L4J 2A2

Dear Children for the Environment

My name is Ari Khan. I am a Grade 9 student at Willfolk Public High School in Vancouver. My classmates and I have started a group called Youth Heroes. We are concerned about loss of habitat for animals across Canada.

I am writing to request an information package on loss of animal habitat in Canada, and want to know how our group can help. If you have a package designed specifically for youth, this would be very helpful, as most of our members are between the ages of 10 and 15.

Thank you for your time. I look forward to hearing from you.

Sincerely,

Ari Khan

Ari Khan

TAKE ACTION! A Guide To Active Citizenship

| **HOME** Preface, Contents | **PART I** How To Get Involved: The Step-By-Step Process | **PART II** The 'How To' Guide |

Thank You Letter

It is important to thank the people who help you. Often, groups lose support simply because they forget to acknowledge the assistance of others. Thanking your supporters will make them more open to helping you again in the future, if necessary. When writing this type of letter, follow these guidelines:

- Be sincere and make the letter personal.
- Refer to the gift or service that was donated.
- Tell the donor how he or she helped your group and cause.
- Express your gratitude and keep in touch with this individual.

PART III
Where You Can Get Involved-
Everywhere!

PART IV
Tackling Social Issues

PART V
Sources And Resources,
End Notes

Sample Thank-You Letter

Anitra Jacobs
Belleview High School
17 Maple Drive
Smithtown, NY
12345 USA

March 31, 20—

Mr. James Chan
T-Shirts R Us
132 Wallace Street
Smithtown, NY
12345 USA

Dear Mr. Chan,

On behalf of the students at Belleview High School, I would like to thank you for your generous donation of 50 fair-trade t-shirts for our rock-a-thon fundraiser.

We had more than 500 people attend the event and raised $1,200, which will go towards building a school for children in Calcutta. These funds will help provide these children with an education and the opportunity to break free from the cycle of poverty.

We thank you again for your help. We will keep you informed about our work.

Gratefully,

Anitra Jacobs
Anitra Jacobs

TAKE ACTION! A Guide To Active Citizenship

HOME Preface, Contents	PART I How To Get Involved: The Step-By-Step Process	PART II The 'How To' Guide

Contacting Government Officials

The following sections will outline the government structures of Canada and the United States. They will inform you as to how to best contact and communicate with the various levels of government you and your group will encounter. Choose to read the section that is most relevant to you.

Contacting Public Officials in Canada

Politicians are elected by adults, but it is their job to represent all people in the area in which they were elected (their constituency), including you. They also make and change laws, so they are good people to contact if you want to make a difference.

In Canada, there are three levels of government: federal, provincial, and municipal. (Territories elect councils that have more limited powers and duties than provincial governments.) Each level of government has specific responsibilities, which are outlined below.

Municipal

Municipal governments are in charge of towns and cities, and usually comprise the following individuals:
- mayor
- councilors (local politicians who help run the town or city)
- school board trustees (representatives on educational matters)

Provincial

Provincial governments are in charge of the provinces. A provincial government consists of the following individuals:
- lieutenant-governor (the monarch's representative in the province)
- premier (leader of the political party with the most support in the provincial legislature)
- cabinet members (act as the chief executives of assigned provincial departments)
- members of the legislative assembly (MLAs) in most of Canada; also called members of provincial parliament (MPPs) in Ontario; members of the national assembly (MNAs) in Québec; and members in the house of assembly (MHAs) in Newfoundland and Labrador (represent provincial constituencies)

PART II > The How To Guide > Writing Letters

PART III
Where You Can Get Involved-
Everywhere!

PART IV
Tackling Social Issues

PART V
Sources And Resources,
End Notes

Federal

The federal government is the government of Canada. The federal government consists of the following:

- monarch (official head of state)
- governor general (the monarch's representative in Canada)
- prime minister (head of government, leader of the majority party in the House of Commons)
- cabinet ministers (act as the chief executives of assigned federal department)
- senators (members appointed by the governor general on the recommendation of the prime minister)
- House of Commons (elected federal assembly)

When contacting government officials, keep in mind that certain powers are reserved for the federal government and other powers have been given to provincial or municipal governments. Sometimes responsibilities are shared. Here is a helpful list of how some of the main powers are distributed:

Provincial Responsibilities

Agriculture
Education
Hospitals
Immigration
Labour and trade unions
Local matters (e.g., highway regulation)
Natural resources
Provincial property and civil rights
Timber and wood
Trade and commerce

Municipal Responsibilities

By-laws for the municipality
Garbage collection
Licensing
Parks and recreation
For the municipality
Public libraries
Recycling programs
Zoning

Federal Responsibilities

Agriculture
Census and statistics
Citizenship
Criminal law
Environment
Foreign affairs
Immigration
Indian (native) affairs
Military and defence
Penitentiaries
Sea coast and inland fisheries
Trade and commerce
Transportation

PART III
Where You Can Get Involved-
Everywhere!

PART IV
Tackling Social Issues

PART V
Sources And Resources,
End Notes

You can also write to politicians and leaders of any other country in the world. To obtain an address and name of a foreign head of state, simply contact the embassy of that country in Ottawa. Ask how the head of state should be addressed in a letter (for example, "Your Majesty..." or "Dear President..."). Also ask for the proper spelling of the person's name.

Writing Letters to Government Officials in Canada

When writing a letter to a head of state, politician, or public official, try to keep in mind the following:

- Address the official using his or her correct title.
- Stick to one issue per letter.
- Do your homework. Make sure you accurately describe the problem or issue, and double-check any facts or statistics you use.
- Speak from your own experience or knowledge.
- Ask the official for her or his views on the situation.
- If you disagree with the point of view of the public official, do so in a polite and respectful manner.

Some titles you may need to know:

- The Right Honourable (then include the full name) for the prime minister of Canada
- The Honourable (then include the full name) for a premier of Canada, cabinet ministers, a member of the House of Commons, a senator, or members of Parliament
- Your Excellency for many heads of state and ambassadors, such as the governor general of Canada.
- Your Honour for judges
- Dear Admiral (General, Captain) for military officials
- Your Majesty for kings and queens
- Your Worship for mayors

Contacting Public Officials in the United States

Politicians are elected by adults, but it is their job to represent all people in the area in which they were elected (their constituency), including you. They also make and change laws, so they are good people to contact if you want to make a difference.

In the United States, there are four levels of government: federal, state, county, and municipal (towns, villages, and cities). Each level of government has specific responsibilities, some of which are outlined below. Note that many of these responsibilities overlap between different levels of government.

Municipal

Municipal governments are in charge of villages, towns and cities, and usually comprise the following individuals:

- mayor or city manager
- councilors, selectmen, supervisors, or commissioners (local politicians who help run the village, town, or city)
- school board trustees (representatives on educational matters)

County

County governments are in charge of counties (subdivision of states). A county government usually consists of the following individuals:

- mayor or county executive
- councilors, supervisors, or commissioners (local politicians who help run the county)

State

State governments are in charge of the states. A state government consists of the following individuals:

- governor
- attorney general (the head of the state's legal department
- senators, representatives, delegates, or assemblymen

PART III
Where You Can Get Involved-
Everywhere!

PART IV
Tackling Social Issues

PART V
Sources And Resources,
End Notes

Federal

The federal government is in charge of the country. It is split up into three branches, the executive branch, the legislative branch, and the judicial branch, which are organized to balance each other in powers and responsibilities. The federal government consists of the following elected officials (plus many more who are appointed by the government):

- president
- vice president
- senators
- representatives

When contacting government officials, keep in mind that certain powers are reserved for the federal government and other powers have been given to state, county, or municipal governments. Sometimes responsibilities are shared. Here is a helpful list of how some of the main powers are distributed:

County Responsibilities

Administering welfare programs
Elections
Public libraries
Maintenance of highways and bridges
Making county laws and setting taxes
Sheriff's department

State Responsibilities

Education
Health
Housing and urban development
Regulations relating to property, industry, business, and public utilities
State police
The state criminal code
Transportation
Working conditions
Welfare

Municipal Responsibilities

By-laws for the municipality
Licensing

Maintenance of roads and public buildings
Parks and recreation
Police department
Public libraries
Waste disposal (garbage collection, sewers, recycling, etc.)
Zoning

Federal Responsibilities

Agriculture
Commerce
Defense
Education
Energy
Environment
Finance
Foreign relations
Health
Housing and urban development
Justice
Labor
Military
Transportation

PART III
Where You Can Get Involved-
Everywhere!

PART IV
Tackling Social Issues

PART V
Sources And Resources,
End Notes

You can also write to politicians and leaders of any other country in the world. To obtain an address and name of a foreign head of state, simply contact the embassy of that country in Washington. Ask how the head of state should be addressed in a letter (for example, "Your Majesty..." or "Dear President..."). Also ask for the proper spelling of the person's name.

Writing Letters to Government Officials in the United States

When writing a letter to a head of state, politician, or public official, try to keep in mind the following:

- Address the official using his or her correct title.
- Stick to one issue per letter.
- Do your homework. Make sure you accurately describe the problem or issue, and double-check any facts or statistics you use.
- Speak from your own experience or knowledge.
- Ask the official for his or her views on the situation.
- If you disagree with the point of view of the public official, do so in a polite and respectful manner.

Some titles you may need to know:

- For the president of the United States, address your letter to "President (then include the full name)," and use the greeting "Dear Mr. (or Madam) President."
- For a former president of the United States, address you letter to "The Honorable (then include the full name)," and use the greeting "Dear Mr. (or Ms.) (then the last name).
- For a U.S. senator, address your letter to "The Honorable" (then include the full name), and use the greeting "Dear Senator (then the last name).
- For a U.S. representative, address your letter to "The Honorable" (then include the full name), and use the greeting "Dear Mr. (or Ms.) (then the last name)."
- For a governor, address your letter to "The Honorable" (then the last name), Governor of (name of state)," and use the greeting "Dear Governor (then the last name)."
- For a mayor, address your letter to "The Honorable" (then include the full name); His (or Her) Honor the Mayor," and use the greeting "Dear Mayor (then the last name)."

TAKE Action! A Guide To Active Citizenship

| **Home** Preface, Contents | **PART I** How To Get Involved: The Step-By-Step Process | **PART II** The 'How To' Guide |

Format for a Letter to a Public Official

Your name
Your full address
Telephone, fax, and
e-mail information

Date the letter

Name of public official
Full address

Dear (name of public official or other title)

- Identify yourself: state your full name, grade, and school.
- State your purpose in writing: Explain why you are writing. If it is about a specific bill or law, make reference to it or state its name or number.
- Express your feelings: Tell the politician what you think about the issue. Explain why the cause is important to you.

State any solutions you or your group have for the problem.

- Explain what you want:
  Tell the official why you are writing. You may want the individual to support or oppose a certain bill or law. You may want him or her to create a law regarding an issue.
- Say "thank you":
  Remember to thank the official and state that you look forward to hearing from him or her.

Sincerely,

Type or print your name
and sign the space above

PART II > The How To Guide > Writing Letters

PART III
Where You Can Get Involved-
Everywhere!

PART IV
Tackling Social Issues

PART V
Sources And Resources,
End Notes

Sample Letter to a Canadian Public Official

Eric LeBlanc
121 Sparrow Way
Saskatoon, SK
Canada S3V 3T4

December 17, 20—

Right Honourable Stephen Harper
Prime Minister's Office
80 Wellington Street
Ottawa, ON
Canada K1A 0A2

Dear Right Honourable Stephen Harper:

My name is Eric LeBlanc and I am a Grade 8 student at Meadowvale School in Saskatoon, Saskatchewan. I am writing to you about the issue of child labour and the exploitation of children in developing countries. I have done a lot of research on the subject and have discovered that there are over 352 million labourers in the world between the ages of 5 and 17.

I believe that child labour is wrong and should be stopped. I am aware that you visit many countries and discuss international trade. I believe that this is a good thing, but please do not forget about the children who are working in hazardous conditions when you sign trade deals. I am a young person also, and I believe that these children deserve a better chance at life.

One way to help these children is for Canada to support the Rugmark label. It is a label indicating that a particular carpet was not made from the exploitation of children.

I look forward to hearing from you. Thank you for your time and consideration.

Sincerely,

Eric LeBlanc
Eric LeBlanc

TAKE ACTION! A Guide To Active Citizenship

| **HOME** Preface, Contents | **PART I** How To Get Involved: The Step-By-Step Process | **PART II** The 'How To' Guide |

Sample Letter to an American Public Official

Judy Summerland
2437 Pinevale Lane
Jamestown, ND
45678 USA

Sept 15, 20—

President Barack Obama
The White House
1600 Pennsylvania Avenue NW
Washington, D.C.
20500 USA

Dear Mr. President,

My name is Judy Summerland and I am a tenth grade student at Jamestown High School in Jamestown, North Dakota. I am writing to you about the horrible issue of land mines. Land mines are dangerous weapons of war that kill and maim innocent civilians both during and long after wars have ended. Through my research, I have learned that in the world today, the United Nations estimates that more than 110 million active mines are scattered in 68 countries.

To save men, women and children from being badly hurt by land mines, I believe that they should be banned. There is a treaty to stop land mines that the United States has not signed. It is called the Convention on the Prohibition of the Use, Stockpiling, Production and Transfer of Anti-Personnel Mines and on Their Destruction.

Since 1997, 151 countries have signed this treaty, and I think that my country should too. I am a young person and I want to stop land mines from hurting other young people and their parents.

I look forward to hearing from you. Thank you for your time and consideration.

Sincerely,

Judy Summerland

Judy Summerland

Letter to the Editor

Most newspapers have an editorial page and it is to this page that readers can write letters about matters that concern them. The newspaper decides which letters to publish according to what it believes will interest the paper's readership. Writing a letter to the editor is a good way to voice your opinion and to educate people in your community about important issues. Many people who read the newspaper read these letters.

The following tips will be useful if you decide to write a letter to the editor:

- Editor contact information is usually listed in the editorial section of the newspaper or in the first few pages of a magazine. You can send your letter by e-mail, fax, or regular mail.
- If you are writing about an article you read in a particular newspaper or magazine, cite the date, title, writer, and subject of the article in your letter. Responding to a recently published article is one of the best ways to increase your chances of your letter being published.
- Keep your letter simple. Make it brief and to the point (or it will not be printed).A short letter is more likely to be read. Do not include unnecessary information that detracts from your letter.
- Do your homework. Make certain that all your facts are accurate. Do not exaggerate. Your credibility will be put to the test. Anyone can respond to or criticize your comments.
- Be polite. Remember that you are representing young people.
- Create a headline. Editors are always looking for short and interesting headlines. Make their job easier by writing the headline yourself.
- Make it personal. Editors are more likely to publish a letter if you use personalexperiences or give personal opinions.
- Proofread, proofread, proofread.
- If you are sending your letter by fax or mail, sign your work. Newspapers require a signature, which legally allows them to print the letter. They may phone you back to ensure that you actually wrote the letter yourself, so include your phone number.
- Do not be discouraged if your letter is not published. Keep trying!

TAKE ACTION! A Guide To Active Citizenship

| **HOME** Preface, Contents | **PART I** How To Get Involved: The Step-By-Step Process | **PART II** The 'How To' Guide |

Format for a Letter to the Editor

Your name
Your full address
Telephone, fax, and e-mail
information

Date the letter

Editor of (newspaper)
Full address and fax number

- Identify yourself
    State your full name, your grade, and school.
- State the purpose of your letter:
    If you are writing in response to an article, mention the date, title, and subject.
Briefly explain your cause and state what you are trying to do to help.
- Express your feelings:
    Express your likes or dislikes about the article you have read. Tell the editor why
    the cause is important to you. Mention any solutions to the problem.
- Say "thank you":
    Always thank the editor for his or her time.

Sincerely,

Type or print your name
and sign in the space
above.

PART III
Where You Can Get Involved-
Everywhere!

PART IV
Tackling Social Issues

PART V
Sources And Resources,
End Notes

Sample Letter to the Editor

Sara Crane
1123 Main Street
Markham, ON
Canada L3P 1G3

June 16, 20—

Markham Times
44 Nelson Street
Markham, ON
Canada L2P 1T9

To the Editor:

My name is Sara Crane. I am in Grade 9 at Markham Collegiate in Markham. I am writing in response to the article "Recycling Stops," which was in your paper on June 2. I am very concerned about the environment and have started a group called Enviro Kids.

I am upset because the article says that the picking up of blue boxes will stop in my area next year due to government cutbacks. This is terrible and means that more waste will end up in huge garbage dumps. Young people will inherit this earth. I believe that we all have a serious responsibility to protect our environment. I believe that the recycling program should be saved and that more recycling and composting programs should be created throughout the country. If we only invested as much money in our environment as we do in industries that create pollution, we would all benefit.

Thank you for your time and consideration.

Sincerely,

SARAH CRANE
Sara Crane

PUBLIC SPEAKING

Speaking is one of the most exciting ways to deliver your message. It can spark enthusiasm, interest, and action from those who hear you. People sometimes feel nervous or afraid to speak in front of groups. What these individuals do not realize, however, is that public speaking is easier when you take the time to practice. It can also be lots of fun.

How to Write a Speech

Writing your speech can be the best part of your public-speaking experience. Putting your ideas on paper gives you the chance to completely think through your ideas before you are in front of an audience.

| **PART III** Where You Can Get Involved- Everywhere! | **PART IV** Tackling Social Issues | **PART V** Sources And Resources, End Notes |

Before you begin writing, however, make certain that you have done your homework. Search the Internet and libraries, interview people, and think of stories from your own experience. For research hints, see the section "Do Your Research" in Part 1, beginning on page 5.

There are three essential components to every speech, as outlined below.

Part 1: The Introduction

- If you have not been introduced by someone, state your name, grade, and school.
- If you have been introduced, you may want to begin with an interesting quote or a shocking statistic to grab the audience's attention.
- State what you will speak about (your main points), why you became involved in your issue, and why it is important to you.

Part 2: The Body of the Speech

- Make it interesting and creative. Provide any facts or statistics that you obtained through researching your subject.
- Share with the audience real-world examples of people affected by the issue.
- Tell a story. You might focus on something that happened to you while working on your issue, or on something that you read about while doing your research.
- Explain what you are trying to accomplish and what the future holds for your cause.

Part 3: The Conclusion

- End the speech by summarizing your main points. The conclusion should be a short statement—a message the audience will remember.
- Briefly explain how audience members can become involved in your campaign. (Ask for action on their part.)
- Inform listeners that you will stay to answer questions after your speech. You may want to have some flyers to hand out.
- Thank the audience for their time and attention.

TAKE ACTION! A Guide To Active Citizenship

| **Home** Preface, Contents | **PART I** How To Get Involved: The Step-By-Step Process | **PART II** The 'How To' Guide |

Stories are sometimes the best way to convey an idea to an audience. You might tell the audience how you first became socially involved, or share with them a funny incident that happened to your group while raising funds. Or, perhaps you could recount the story of a young person you have met who has been negatively affected by the problem or social issue you are trying to change. Try to be descriptive, using words that draw pictures in the minds of your listeners.

Posture is another important element in public speaking. Your presentation must not only sound good, it must also look good. Often, your delivery is just as important as what you are saying. Standing correctly, smiling, and appearing relaxed (even if you are nervous) are key components of a successful speech.

Energy can be contagious. If you are energetic and full of enthusiasm about your subject, you just might spark that same passion in your listeners. Demonstrate how much you care about your issue, adjusting your energy level to suit the audience. If you are speaking to fellow students or to a younger audience, you may have to heighten the intensity of your presentation in order to hold their attention.

Ask for action. This is something that many speakers forget to do. If you are speaking about an important social issue, tell your listeners how they, too, can become active in your campaign. Offer them three avenues to involvement: (1) A simple action, like signing a petition at the back of the room; (2) A more difficult action, such as donating $10 to your cause; (3) A significant action, such as learning more about the issue and telling people at their school, work, or place of worship about the problem.

<table>
<tr><td>

PART III
Where You Can Get Involved-
Everywhere!

</td><td>

PART IV
Tackling Social Issues

</td><td>

PART V
Sources And Resources,
End Notes

</td></tr>
</table>

Know your audience. To whom will you be speaking? You do not want to give the same speech to students in Grade 5 as would to members of Parliament or Congress. Try to adapt your speech to your audience. For example, if you are speaking to parents, you may want to encourage them to get their children involved in the issue.

Interesting facts and statistics add credibility to what you are saying and help to convey the importance of your issue. Did you know that half the people in this world have never made a telephone call? Or, that over three billion people in the world live on less than five dollars a day. It's true! Remember, never make up facts or statistics and make certain you obtain them from reliable sources.

No reading! Reading shows the audience that you are not prepared to give your speech. Having notes or cue cards listing major points is fine, but the most powerful presentations are delivered from the heart. Make certain, however, that you take the time to familiarize yourself with the main ideas in your speech. Then practice, practice, practice.

Give from the heart. This is the most important thing to remember when you speak. Why are you passionate about your issue? Who are the people you are trying to help? Believe in yourself and in your ability to make a difference.

The Do's and Don'ts of Delivering a Speech

One of the secrets to giving a great speech is to have fun. Try to enjoy speaking to your audience about the social issue that inspires you. Here are a few other suggestions to keep in mind:

Do's

- Wait for the noise in the room to die down before you begin.
- Make eye contact; look at your audience and smile.
- Direct your speech to the entire audience, not just to those people immediately in front of you or on one side of the room.
- Wear comfortable clothes that are appropriate for the presentation.
- Speak slowly, loudly, and clearly.

Don'ts

- Don't clasp your hands, hold them behind your back, or put them in your pockets. You may want to hold a pen in your hand instead.
- Don't exaggerate your hand movements.
- Don't move your feet or shift your weight from one leg to the other too often. Doing so can distract the audience.
- Don't chew gum.
- Don't read your speech. Some speakers memorize their entire speech, while others periodically refer to speaking notes written on index cards, which is acceptable.

Tip!

Tips for Memorizing

- *Read your speech over and over again. Read it silently. Read it out loud. Read it to your family, friends, or even your pet.*
- *Record your speech on tape and listen to it when you have some free time: on your way to school, before bed, or while brushing your teeth.*
- *Write out your speech several times. Eventually, you will no longer need your notes.*
- *Have someone videotape you giving your speech and play it back so that you can see what the audience will see.*

PART II > The How To Guide > Public Speaking

| **PART III** Where You Can Get Involved- Everywhere! | **PART IV** Tackling Social Issues | **PART V** Sources And Resources, End Notes |

1. SMILE.

2. CHIN UP.

3. KEEP YOUR SHOULDERS RELAXED.

4. YOU MAY WANT TO HOLD A PEN IF YOU TEND TO PUT YOUR HANDS IN YOUR POCKETS.

5. DO NOT MOVE YOUR HIPS TOO MUCH.

6. YOU MAY WANT TO STAND WITH ONE FOOT SLIGHTLY FORWARD.

7. KEEP YOUR FEET SECURE ON THE GROUND AND DO NOT "DANCE."

Sample Speech

Ladies and Gentlemen,

(INTRODUCTION)

My name is Catherine Wong. I am 13 years old and in eighth grade at Parkview Middle School. I am a member of the group Kids Helping the Homeless. We are a group of young people working to help the less fortunate in our community. Did you know that our homeless population has grown by more than 4 per cent every year for the past five years? Did you know that 40 per cent of the people who are out on the streets are under 20 years of age, many coming from broken and abusive homes? In my opinion, however, the saddest fact is that the programs that are supposed to help the homeless are about to have their funding cut by City Council. We do not think that this is fair!

(BODY and STORY)

Homeless people are just like you and me. Last night, when you and I were tucked into our warm beds, they slept on the cold, hard pavement of our city streets. When our school went to visit the local food bank, we met homeless people in line for baskets of food, and realized just how lucky we were. One woman I met, named Sandra, had been living on the streets for the past two years. She had a dog named Benny who was very cute and friendly. She told me that because she had her dog, which she kept for company, she was not allowed into the shelters. Sandra ended up on the streets because she was abused at home. Out on her own, she could not find work. She was really a nice person, funny and interesting. I felt really sad knowing that she and Benny would not have a home to go to that night. I did some research and found out that there are not enough homeless shelters to accommodate the number of people currently on the streets. I also found out that two homeless people died on the streets of our city last year because of the cold. I don't think that this is fair, do you?

Our group, Kids Helping Kids, is trying to make a difference. We are helping our community by collecting old coats, blankets, and sleeping bags to give to shelters. We are also making food baskets so that homeless people can eat a nourishing meal. As well, we are asking City Council to pass a bill that will give more money to the construction of shelters for the homeless.

(CONCLUSION)

Today, however, we are asking for your help. You can do one of three things: (1) Sign our petition at the back of the room, asking City Council to pass a bill regarding the homeless; (2) Call or write your elected officials at the national level and tell them you think the homeless problem should be an urgent issue on the national agenda; (3) Donate $20 to help make a "cold kit" to give to homeless people during the winter months. But, most importantly, please be nice to homeless people.

If you would like more information or are interested in getting involved in our campaign, please let me know. I would be happy to answer any questions. Thank you for your time.

PART II > The How To Guide > How To Do A Survey

PART III
Where You Can Get Involved-
Everywhere!

PART IV
Tackling Social Issues

PART V
Sources And Resources,
End Notes

SOUND BYTES: OK!

"Whenever I go out to give a speech, whether it's to 10 or 1000 people, I get a little nervous feeling in my stomach. I have simply learned that this just shows you care about the speech, and that feeling a little nervous is a good thing."

Jason Apostolopoulos (b.1987) Free The Children speaker

HOW TO DO A SURVEY

Sometimes you need to know what people think about an issue or an idea. For example, you might want to find out how many people would attend a particular event before you go to the trouble of organizing it. Or, you might want to know how many people are affected by a certain problem in your community and how they feel about the solution your team has come up with.

A survey is an excellent tool for
* determining public opinion
* gathering information
* raising awareness about an issue

Surveys can also help you to identify opposition to your cause or, alternatively, help you gather support for it. You might find people who agree with your solutions to a social problem and are interested in joining your team. Conducting a survey can change your perspective about an issue, and help you to develop a broader and more informed point of view.

TAKE ACTiON! A Guide To Active Citizenship

Home	PART I	PART II
Preface, Contents	How To Get Involved: The Step-By-Step Process	The 'How To' Guide

Four Steps to a Successful Survey

Step 1: Do Your Homework

- Surveys require a lot of work and co-operation from others, so you should only consider conducting a survey if you have a clear purpose in mind. Do you feel that you need specific information from your classmates or community members in order to effectively tackle your social issue? Is there any other way—for example, through research—that you could obtain the type of information you need before you begin? Even if you do decide that a survey is necessary, it is important to conduct some preliminary research before you begin.
- Think about the people who will be answering your questions. Do you want to survey a specific group, or can your questions be answered by anyone?

Step 2: Write a Questionnaire

- Each person who responds to your survey needs a separate questionnaire (a copy of the questions on which to record the answers).
- Write the title of the survey at the top of the questionnaire.
- Provide the name and address of your group so people can return their questionnaire. Thank them for their time.
- Indicate the purpose of your survey.
- State what you intend to do with the results.
- Choose the format for your questions: short answer, check-off lists, yes or no questions, statements requiring a degree of assent (for example, strongly agree, agree, disagree, strongly disagree). It is best to include a variety of questions in your survey, as well as instructions for how to answer them.
- Leave space for answers to be filled in.
- Try to avoid questions that require long answers as they discourage people from responding and can be difficult to interpret.
- Limit the number of questions in your survey. Only ask questions that are important to your research. If the survey can be filled out quickly, more people will be inclined to respond.

PART II > The How To Guide > How To Do A Survey

| **PART III** Where You Can Get Involved- Everywhere! | **PART IV** Tackling Social Issues | **PART V** Sources And Resources, End Notes |

Step 3: Conduct Your Survey

- Surveys can be done in person, by phone, or by mail. Some people dislike being called at home, and some will be reluctant to respond to your letters. So, the best way to do a survey is the direct way: in person. When you can tell people face-to-face how much you appreciate their opinion, it will be more difficult for them to walk away.
- You can conduct surveys in public places, such as your school, neighborhood community center, or mall, but you may have to obtain permission in advance. You may need to have a teacher or a parent/guardian with you to supervise. (Note: Never go door-to-door without having an adult accompany you.)
- Distribute copies of the questionnaire to as many people as possible.
- Take plenty of copies of your survey and plenty of pens. There is nothing worse than running out of supplies just when you spot a huge group of people coming your way.
- Remember to be friendly and polite. Some people will not be as willing to participate in your survey as others. Keep your cool, thank them anyway, and move onto the next candidate.
- Some people might disagree with the ideas in your survey. Use this opportunity to find out what they would suggest as an alternative.

TIP!

The more people who answer your survey, the more accurate it will be.

TAKe ACtiON! A Guide To Active Citizenship

| **Home** Preface, Contents | **PART I** How To Get Involved: The Step-By-Step Process | **PART II** The 'How To' Guide |

Step 4: Assess the Results

- Once you have received as many questionnaires as possible, tabulate the results, organize the information using charts and tables, and write a report.
- When analyzing your results, think about how they reflect the group of people who participated in your survey. Did an equal number of males and females answer your questions? Were they of various ages and ethnic backgrounds? Where they from different geographic locations? The answer does not have to be yes, just be sure to consider this aspect of your survey when interpreting its results.
- Let other people know what you have discovered through your survey and why it is important. Set up an information booth or use the results of your survey in a flyer or poster. How do people react to your findings? Motivate them to take action and join your team.

PART II > The How To Guide > How To Do A Survey

PART III
Where You Can Get Involved-
Everywhere!

PART IV
Tackling Social Issues

PART V
Sources And Resources,
End Notes

Sample Survey

Please answer the following questions by putting a check mark in the appropriate space. When you are finished, please return this survey to Kim Chong.

Please check one of the following:

Male _____ Female _____

Age: _____ under 10   _____ 12-15 _____16-18

            _____ 18-25   _____ 26-30 _____ 30+

1. Have you ever taken action (or helped) on a social issue (environment, poverty, education etc.)? Check one.

   Yes _____   No _____

2. If yes, in what types of social action did you get involved? Please check all those that apply to you.

   ____ School (education)   ____ Human Rights

   ____ Environmental   ____ Children's Rights

   ____ Community (homelessness, poverty)   ____ Other (please specify)

   _____

TAKE ACTION! A Guide To Active Citizenship

Home	PART I	PART II
Preface, Contents	How To Get Involved: The Step-By-Step Process	The 'How To' Guide

Survey Cont'd

3. Do you belong to an organization working on social or human rights issues?

   Yes _____   No _____

4. If yes, is this organization run by adults or young people?

   Adults _____   Young people _____

5. Would you like to become involved in an organization working for children's rights?

   Yes _____   No _____

6. I believe that most young people want to become involved in a social issue. Do you... (check one).

   _____ Strongly agree   _____ Strongly disagree

   _____ Agree   _____ Do not know   _____ Disagree

PART II > The How To Guide > How To Do A Survey

| **PART III** Where You Can Get Involved- Everywhere! | **PART IV** Tackling Social Issues | **PART V** Sources And Resources, End Notes |

Survey Cont'd

7. Why do you think that young people do not become involved in social issues or human rights issues? Check as many as you like.

_____ Do not know an issue _____ More interested in sports

_____ Cannot find an issue _____ More interested in television

_____ No adult support _____ Other (please specify) _____

8. Can you name any organizations dealing with social and human rights run by young people between the ages of 10 and 18?

_____

_____

_____

9. We need more groups or organizations dealing with social issues in which youth (ages 10-18) have a voice in decision-making. Check one.

_____ Yes _____ No

Thank you for taking the time to complete our survey.

TAKE ACTION! A Guide To Active Citizenship

| **Home** Preface, Contents | **PART I** How To Get Involved: The Step-By-Step Process | **PART II** The 'How To' Guide |

HOW TO WRITE A PETITION

If you are concerned about something, and you think other people share your point of view, you can use a petition to gather support for your idea. A petition is a powerful tool for a community. It lets decision-makers know that a lot of people are concerned about a particular issue. It asks them to take action to bring about change.

You can use a petition to make change at your school, in your community, or at the local, provincial (Canada), state (United States) or national levels of government.

The following pages will show you how to do this in both Canada and the United States.

The steps to writing an effective petition are as follows:

Give it a title

To: To whom are you giving the petition?

From: Identify your group. Are you all from the same school? From the same community? From an organization?

State your purpose: State the reason for submitting a petition and supply the facts to support your submission.

Make your request: The petition must include a request. What do you want the person(s) receiving the petition to do to solve the problem?

Collect signatures: Collect as many signatures as you can. Be sure to get a full address beside each name, including city and postal code.

Present your petition: Present your petition to a person who will listen to you and who has the power to make changes.

PART II > The How To Guide > How To Write A Petition

| **PART III** Where You Can Get Involved-Everywhere! | **PART IV** Tackling Social Issues | **PART V** Sources And Resources, End Notes |

Sample Petition

Let's Have Lunch Outside

To: Mr. Stedwill, Principal of Hillcrest School
From: Students of Hillcrest School

We, the students of Hillcrest School, would like to be able to eat lunch outside during the spring and the fall. It gets extremely hot inside the classrooms and they are very uncomfortable. It is very difficult to concentrate in class during the afternoon. We would like to eat our lunch outside in the fresh air. We would eat on school grounds and would follow the appropriate rules regarding clean-up.

Name	Grade	Homeroom
_____	_____	_____
_____	_____	_____
_____	_____	_____
_____	_____	_____
_____	_____	_____
_____	_____	_____
_____	_____	_____

TAKE ACTION! A Guide To Active Citizenship

| **Home**
Preface, Contents | **PART I**
How To Get Involved:
The Step-By-Step Process | **PART II**
The 'How To' Guide |

Tip!

If there is more than one page to your petition, you must rewrite the purpose and request of the petition at the top of each page.

How to Write a Petition to the Federal Government of Canada

In preparing a petition in Canada for the federal government, there are very specific rules you must follow:

- If you are sending your petition to the federal government, you must submit it to your member of Parliament (MP) so that it can be read in the House of Commons. It is a good idea to contact the member of Parliament before making your petition to ask if the MP would agree to present it to the House of Commons. Once it has been presented, the government must send a response to the MP within 45 days.
- Petitions can be handwritten, printed, typed, or photocopied on paper measuring 21.5 cm x 28 cm (8.5" x 11") or 21.5 cm x 35.5 cm (8.5" x 14"). In other words, use letter-sized or legal-sized paper.
- Always be polite and use appropriate language.
- Do not attach any other documents to the petition, such as maps, pictures, or newspaper articles.
- The petition must be about an issue for which the federal government has authority. Make sure you send your petition to the right level of government. The section "Writing Letters" includes information on writing to government officials and outlines how the areas of power are divided among the municipal, provincial, and federal governments (see page 47).
- Collect as many signatures as possible. At least 25 signatures are required to have your petition read in the House of Commons.
- The petition must contain a request, called a prayer, for Parliament to take some action (or refrain from taking some action) or to fix a problem. A statement of opinion alone cannot be received as a petition. The petition must not demand or insist that Parliament do something. The prayer should be clear and to the point.
- The petitioner's address must be written directly on the petition. The petitioner may give his or her full home address or simply the city and province.

PART II > The How To Guide > How To Write A Petition

| **PART III** Where You Can Get Involved- Everywhere! | **PART IV** Tackling Social Issues | **PART V** Sources And Resources, End Notes |

Format for a Petition to the House of Commons

1. Identify yourself.
   We, the undersigned, (identify who the petitioners are)
   - citizens or residents of Canada.
   - residents of the province of...
   - residents of the city/town of...
   - students from _____ School
2. State your purpose.
   Draw the attention of the House to the following:

THAT,

State the reason why you are submitting a petition to the House of Commons and supply facts to support your statement.

3. Make your request.
The petition must have a request. In government language, this is called a prayer to Parliament to take action. The prayer should be clear and to the point.

THEREFORE, your petitioners request that Parliament...
Make your request to the government. State what actions the government should or should not take to solve the problem.

4. Signatures.

TAKE ACTION! A Guide To Active Citizenship

| **Home** Preface, Contents | **PART I** How To Get Involved: The Step-By-Step Process | **PART II** The 'How To' Guide |

TIP!

If you want a member of Parliament to introduce your petition in the House of Commons, do not allow any pencil, pen, stamps, or other marks to be made anywhere on the petition pages. Only names, addresses, and signatures located in the appropriate places will be acknowledged. If doodle marks of any kind appear on a given page, that entire page of your petition will be disqualified and all of the signatures on that page will be subtracted from your final count.

PART II > The How To Guide > How To Write A Petition

PART III
Where You Can Get Involved-
Everywhere!

PART IV
Tackling Social Issues

PART V
Sources And Resources,
End Notes

Sample Petition to the House of Commons

A Petition to the House of Commons

Students of Canal Street School, Ottawa, Ontario.

We, the undersigned, students from Canal Street School, draw the attention of the House to the following:

THAT much of the food imported into Canada is produced under conditions which undervalue producers work and result in low incomes for struggling farmers;
THAT such practices perpetuate global inequalities and rural poverty;
THAT proper regulation and legislation can ensure that food imported into Canada is fair trade certified;
THEREFORE, your petitioners request that Parliament support legislation for the creation of enforceable, Canada-wide standards for fair and ethical trade in imported food.

Printed Name   Signature   Address

TAKE ACTiON! A Guide To Active Citizenship

Home	PART I	PART II
Preface, Contents	How To Get Involved: The Step-By-Step Process	The 'How To' Guide

How to Write a Petition to the United States Government

A petition to the government should be written just like any other petition, stating who you are, the purpose of your petition, what you want the government to do about the problem, and your list of signatures. Addresses should also be included for all the signatures. Make sure you send your petition to the right level of government (see page 51 for lists of basic responsibilities for the different levels of government in the United States). If you want to petition the federal government on a national or international issue, you can send your petition straight to the White House, but it will probably get more attention if you address it to your local member of Congress or the head of a particular committee or department.

- Print your petition on letter-sized or legal-sized paper.
- The petition should be clear and to the point.
- Always be polite and use appropriate language.
- Do not attach any other documents to the petition, such as maps, pictures, or newspaper articles.
- Collect as many signatures as possible.
- The petitioner's address must be written directly on the petition. The petitioner may give his or her full home address or simply the city and state.

PART III
Where You Can Get Involved-
Everywhere!

PART IV
Tackling Social Issues

PART V
Sources And Resources,
End Notes

Format for a Petition to the United States Government

1. Identify yourself.
   We, the undersigned, (identify who the petitioners are)
   - citizens or residents of the United States.
   - residents of the state of...
   - residents of the city/town of...
   - students from _____ School

2. State your purpose.
   Draw the attention of the government to the following:

THAT,

State the reason why you are submitting a petition to the government and supply facts to support your statement.

3. Make your request.
The petition must have a request. The petition should be clear and to the point.

THEREFORE, your petitioners request that...
State what actions the government should or should not take to solve the problem.

4. Signatures.

Sample Petition to the United States Congress

A Petition to the Congress of the United States

Students of Hillcrest School, Milton, Massachusetts.

We, the undersigned, students from Hillcrest School, draw the attention of Congress to the following:

THAT incidents of accidental shootings are becoming more and more frequent, exemplified by the recent school shooting at Barclays Public School;
THAT each incident of misuse of guns can hurt the public;
THAT proper legislation can prevent these accidents;
THEREFORE, your petitioners request that Congress support legislation for stronger gun control.

Printed Name   Signature   Address

PART III Where You Can Get Involved- Everywhere!	**PART IV** Tackling Social Issues	**PART V** Sources And Resources, End Notes

HOW TO RAISE PUBLIC AWARENESS AND SUPPORT

This section outlines the skills and tools you need to get your message out to the public accurately and effectively. You will learn the following:

- How to make great posters, flyers, and pamphlets.
- How to write an effective press release for newspapers, radio, and television.
- How to make a public service announcement.
- How to give an interview that is so effective it just might make it on the evening news.
- How to create a user-friendly website.

How to Use the Media

Every time you pick up a newspaper, watch TV, or turn on the radio, you are being influenced by the media. But the media can be one of the most powerful tools when you are trying to get an important message out to the public. For example, you can spend three weeks giving 10 speeches throughout your community and potentially reach 1,000 people. Or, you may reach the same number of people, if not many more, simply by giving an interview on your local television station. You can use the media to help further your cause.

The word "media" is actually the plural form of the word "medium," defined as a means through which something else acts. The media are a tool for getting your message across and include the following:

- posters, flyers, and pamphlets
- newspapers
- public service announcements (PSAs)
- radio
- television
- the Internet

The Basics

Any time you send a message to the public, it is a good idea to imagine that you are hearing the message for the very first time. Make certain that you include all important information. For example, telling people about your event will not help you accomplish your goal if you forget to tell them where or when the event is taking place.

TAKE ACTION! A Guide To Active Citizenship

| **Home** Preface, Contents | **PART I** How To Get Involved: The Step-By-Step Process | **PART II** The 'How To' Guide |

When you are communicating with the media, be sure to address the five Ws + H:

_ Who?
_ What?
_ When?
_ Where?
_ Why?
_ How?

Tip!

When working with the media, always be polite, professional, and use appropriate language.

PART II > The How To Guide > How To Raise Public Awareness And Support

| **PART III**
Where You Can Get Involved-
Everywhere! | **PART IV**
Tackling Social Issues | **PART V**
Sources And Resources,
End Notes |

Using Posters, Flyers, and Pamphlets Effectively

These are all easy, inexpensive ways of using the media to your advantage. The more care you take in designing them, the more effective they can be.

Posters

Making posters is an easy way to advertise, advance your cause, and raise awareness. Here are some techniques for effective poster design:

- Make them large, colorful, eye-catching, and easy to read from a distance.
- Include the name of your organization and necessary contact information.
- Consider including some kind of picture or group logo.
- Post them in places where they will have the most exposure to your intended audience.

Flyers

Flyers are simple handouts used to inform people about events. They are designed to reach large numbers of people and can be easily distributed throughout entire communities.

- Make one flyer, proofread it, and then, when you are confident it is free of errors, photocopy as many as you need. Consider using recycled paper (even though it sometimes costs a little more). See the section "How to Raise Funds" beginning on page 100 for tips on how to get copies made free of charge.
- Do not associate your cause with junk mail. For example, do not put your flyer on the type of bright colors that you get in your mailbox every day and that often get put into the recycling bin without being read. Copy your flyer on relatively good quality white or off-white paper, rather than on bright pink, yellow, or green paper.
- Put your flyers in mailboxes or leave stacks of them in stores or at the information desks of libraries and community centers, after you have obtained permission to do so.

Pamphlets

Having pamphlets for distribution is a wonderful way to educate people about your group and its mandate. Pamphlets are often made from a standard sheet of paper folded into three panels, with different pieces of information on each panel. You should include the following information in your pamphlet:

- Background information on your group.
- Information on the problem you are trying to solve. Consider including two or three key facts or statistics.
- The projects your group has started or is hoping to support.
- Information on how others can get involved and help.
- Contact information for people who wish to get in touch with your group. Once your pamphlet is designed and printed, the next question you have to think about is how you are going to get it into the hands of the people who will be interested in your cause. Here are some helpful suggestions for the distribution of pamphlets:
- Leave pamphlets at the community information desk at your local library or community center after you have obtained permission to do so.
- Request permission to hand out the pamphlets to your peers and friends at your school, place of worship, or at an extra-curricular activity.
- If you give any speeches or presentations to groups, have pamphlets on hand for people who might be interested in more information.
- If you plan to distribute the pamphlets door-to-door, or to people whom you do not know, take the necessary safety precautions. For example, work in groups and have an adult supervise.

How to Write a Press Release

Are you organizing an important event? Are you planning a big fundraiser for your community, or an information session about your social issue for the entire school? How can you tell the press about what is taking place?

The answer is that you can communicate with the press using a press release. This is one way businesses, charities, and governments inform the press about issues that are important to them. By sending a press release to the local media, you can tell the press about your event and obtain valuable free publicity for your cause if the press profiles what you are doing.

PART II > The How To Guide > How To Raise Public Awareness And Support

PART III
Where You Can Get Involved-
Everywhere!

PART IV
Tackling Social Issues

PART V
Sources And Resources,
End Notes

Here are some hints on how to write a press release:

- Follow the sample outlined on the next page as closely as possible.
- Give the press plenty of advanced notice. If a reporter only hears about your event at the last minute, he or she may not have time to attend.
- Fax or e-mail your press release to the reporter three times: (1) One week before your event; (2) 48 hours before your event; and (3) 24 hours before your event. You may want to send it out fewer times to small newspapers, or if you have already heard back from the reporter confirming his or her attendance. You may also want to update your press release if, for example, you have been able to confirm the appearance of a local celebrity at your event, or if other additional information is now available.
- Ensure your press release looks professional. Check your information for accuracy and have someone edit it for spelling and grammar. Finally, double-space your press release so that it is easy to read.
- Keep it short and to the point. Include important information and make it interesting, but avoid including too many details. Doing so might lead the reporter to think he or she can write the story without having to attend your event.
- Write your press release in the third person so that it sounds impartial.
- Include the contact name and phone number of one person in your group. Consider borrowing someone's cell phone for a few days leading up to the event and for the day of the event itself. This will make it easier for reporters to reach you. Make certain, however, that you turn off the cell phone during class.
- At the end of your press release, include the following symbol: -30-. The press recognizes -30- as a signal that the end of the article has been reached.

TAKE ACTION!   A Guide To Active Citizenship

| **Home**
Preface, Contents | **PART I**
How To Get Involved:
The Step-By-Step Process | **PART II**
The 'How To' Guide |

Format for a Press Release

PRESS RELEASE

Title of the Press Release
(make it sound interesting)

Contact person's name
Full address
Telephone and fax numbers
Cell phone number (if you have one)
E-mail address

Date of the press release

1. State your purpose/describe your event.

   Clearly express the purpose of the press release and what your event involves. The first sentence is the most important. It should be interesting and contain newsworthy information.

2. Identify yourself or your group.

   State who you are (your name, age, school, etc.) and who you represent (the name of your group).

3. Location, times, and dates.

   Describe when and where the event will take place.

4. Other information.

   Include any other important details, such as the confirmed appearance of a local celebrity, or the goal of your event (for example, the amount of money you hope to raise).

5. End note.
   If the press release is 'more' than one page, write more at the bottom of each page. On the last page, write '-30-' at the bottom to indicate that you are finished. This will make you look professional.

PART II > The How To Guide > How To Raise Public Awareness And Support

PART III
Where You Can Get Involved-
Everywhere!

PART IV
Tackling Social Issues

PART V
Sources And Resources,
End Notes

Sample Press Release

PRESS RELEASE

KIDS TAKE TO THE STREETS

Judy Steinberg
321 Nelson Street
Georgetown, SC
29440 USA
Tel: 843-555-9890
Fax: 843-555-3434
Kidshelpingkids@hotmail.com

October 25, 20—

     On November 3, the youth of Georgetown will be taking to the streets to participate in a 10-mile walkathon to raise funds for cystic fibrosis research.

     The event is being organized by the ninth grade students of South Ridge High in Georgetown. The students of the school have started a group called Kids Helping Kids and are trying to reach a goal of $5,000 to donate to cystic fibrosis research.

     The walkathon will start at 9:00 a.m. on Saturday, November 3, in front of the town library. William Lawson, local social activist, as well as a player for the Carolina Panthers football team, will be speaking at the opening ceremonies.

     Pledge forms are available at all local libraries or by downloading one from our website. Spectators are most welcome. It is estimated that over 1,000 young people will participate and 'take to the streets.'

-30-

Here are some hints for contacting the press:

- Carefully pick the event that you want the press to cover, because they will probably only cover one or two of your events per year.
- Most press people are not interested, for example, in simply covering a car wash for charity. Make certain that the event you want covered is important and newsworthy enough to attract the press. Or, you can make your car wash more interesting to the press by, perhaps, inviting and confirming the attendance of the mayor and other city councilors, and adding the promise of a water fight at the end of the day (with the consent of the invitees, of course).

PART II > **The How To Guide** > **How To Raise Public Awareness And Support**

| **PART III**
Where You Can Get Involved-
Everywhere! | **PART IV**
Tackling Social Issues | **PART V**
Sources And Resources,
End Notes |

- The person who will probably read your press release is an editor. It is this person's responsibility to decide whether your event is worth covering and, if so, to assign a specific reporter to the story. Editors read thousands of press releases every year. Think of ways you can make your event and press release different and special. Remember, you usually have only about 30 seconds to grab the attention of the editors who will read your press release.

Tip!

Pick a convenient time for the media to attend. If you are trying to attract the local TV news, for example, the reporter may have a 5:00 p.m. deadline in order to have the event broadcast on the 6:00 p.m. news. Therefore, schedule your event for the early afternoon.

Now that you have your press release, to whom should you send it? How do you find and contact the people who would be interested in your cause? Here are some helpful hints:

- Research the news organizations that make up your local media. This may include TV stations, a number of newspapers, magazines, radio stations, and Internet sites. You may want to ask your teacher or parents/guardians for their advice.
- It is more difficult (but not impossible) to attract people from non-community media to cover local events. If you can attract a well-known celebrity to your event, or if you plan to do something special and unique in your campaign, you may want to contact larger media groups to cover your event.
- Collect all the names and phone numbers of the media you want to contact.
- Call the main phone line of each media outlet on your list and ask for the name, phone number, and fax number of the person who covers community news. Be prepared to briefly describe your event to the receptionist.
- Contact the media people first by fax, and then possibly follow up with a phone call. Community reporters often enjoy covering events that young people organize because they are different, unique, and frequently fun.

TAKE ACTION! A Guide To Active Citizenship

Home	PART I	PART II
Preface, Contents	How To Get Involved: The Step-By-Step Process	The 'How To' Guide

- If you are holding a fundraiser for an established organization that is active in your local community, such as the Cancer Society or the Humane Society, consider asking them for help with publicity. They may be willing to send your press release to some of their media contacts.
- Believe in yourself and be confident.

To ensure your event goes as smoothly and professionally as possible, follow some of these helpful hints for dealing with the media:

Before the media arrives...

* Designate one person in your group as the media's main contact person. This person should be well informed, able to answer questions, and supplied with written information to hand out.
* If the conference or event is indoors, use a room that will look filled even if the turnout is small.
* Have a media kit on hand to give to reporters. A media kit is essentially the same as a press release kit, with perhaps a few more items added. This kit should contain the following:
  - a copy of your media release
  - contact names and phone numbers of key people in your group
  - information about the issue, such as facts and statistics
  - brief biography of the speaker(s) or people of note, such as local politicians or celebrities, who will be at the event.
  - photographs, charts, newsletters, or pamphlets, if appropriate. You may want to create some of these specifically for your event.
  - endorsements, quotes, and comments (make certain that they are accurate)
* Have all necessary material on hand and all equipment checked to ensure it works.
* Think of any questions you might be asked and have an idea of how you will answer those questions.
* Be confident. Remember why you organized the event and why you are passionate about your issue. Be energetic and demonstrate the power of your commitment and dedication.
* Look professional and neat.
* Be honest—use only correct statistics and facts. Make certain that you have done your homework and know as much as possible about your issue.

PART II > The How To Guide > How To Raise Public Awareness And Support

| **PART III** Where You Can Get Involved-Everywhere! | **PART IV** Tackling Social Issues | **PART V** Sources And Resources, End Notes |

* Use proper English, not slang, when speaking.

* Do not chew gum.

* Smile.

Television is one of the most effective ways to publicize your campaign. It affords you the opportunity to educate thousands (if not millions) of viewers about your issue. Whether you are interviewed on the local community show or on a national
talk show, there are a number of things to remember in order to make your television appearance a success. Follow these guidelines when being interviewed on TV:

* Always look towards the interviewer and never into the camera itself when
answering questions. Pretend that the camera person is invisible.

* Do not wear striped clothing or any clothing that is solid white or black. Stripes
and solid white and black do not look good on TV. Wear something colorful and youthful.

*   Try to keep your answers short. Short sentences, called 'sound bites,' are catchy and powerful statements that work well on television. An example of a sound bite is "youth are not only the leaders of tomorrow, they are also the leaders of today!"
*   Identify beforehand three important components of your event or cause that you want to have broadcast to the world.
*   Take a deep breath before you answer the questions. This will help to prevent you from saying "ummmmm" before you respond.
*   Ask the interviewer when the interview will be aired on TV.
*   Make sure your friends or family record the program. You cannot count on receiving copies from the television station.
*   Try to relax and enjoy yourself.

Below are some typical questions the media ask when covering events organized by young people. You may want to think about possible answers to these questions before the event.
*   What is this event about? What are you trying to accomplish?
*   Why is this issue important to you?
*   What has been your greatest challenge thus far in your work?
*   There is the common idea that young people only want to hang around malls and play video games. Do you agree? What makes your group different?
*   What is the next planned event for your cause?

SOUND BYTES: `OK!`

   "Concentrate on where you want to go, not on what you fear."

Anthony Robbins (b. 1960) Motivational speaker

PART III
Where You Can Get Involved-
Everywhere!

PART IV
Tackling Social Issues

PART V
Sources And Resources,
End Notes

*   What can people do to find out more information about your issue or get
     involved in your campaign?

*   What message do you want to give to the young people who will be watching or
     reading about this interview?

On the next two pages is a sample interview:

TAKE ACTION! A Guide To Active Citizenship

| **HOME** Preface, Contents | **PART I** How To Get Involved: The Step-By-Step Process | **PART II** The 'How To' Guide |

If I Were Mayor...

Craig Kielburger, Child Labor Activist

"If I were Mayor" first appeared in the Thornhill Post, March 1998. Reprinted with permission.

As Mayor what leader or prominent person would you try to emulate?

I liked Barbara Hall's style. It was amazing how she found the time to attend so many community events and how at ease she was with everyone in the city. She was a people's mayor.

Who would be your biggest supporters?

Young people, although they couldn't vote. I would make sure that they would have opportunities to participate in all city activities and to have a voice in issues which affect them.

What would your campaign slogan be?
"Yes, We Can"

Your campaign song?
"It's a Small World"

Write the first line of your acceptance speech:
It takes a village to raise a child. It also takes a child to help raise a village.

Once in office, what would be your first action?

To create a volunteer youth core program with a stipend for young people who are unemployed or underemployed. I would encourage them to use their energy, enthusiasm and idealism to help improve our city and our communities.

Who would be your closest advisor?

I would need more than one close advisor. When you look at the diversity of the people of Toronto and the influence the city has nationally and internationally, I think that the mayor has to be very careful to have advisors who reflect the complexity of the city. Young people would be well represented.

What three things would you have on your desk?

A picture of my family, my computer and my backgammon game and a special bed for my dog, Muffin, under my desk.

How would your wardrobe change?
I would wear all of my Toronto T-shirts - a different one each day, Maple Leafs, Blue Jays, Raptors, Kids Help Phone, etc. I would inaugurate a casual day across the entire city one day a week at all places of employment with $1 going to local charities.

What is one thing about Toronto that you would most like to change?

I'd like to see more people participate in the decisions being made. I would install a huge

PART II > The How To Guide > How To Raise Public Awareness And Support

PART III
Where You Can Get Involved-
Everywhere!

PART IV
Tackling Social Issues

PART V
Sources And Resources,
End Notes

suggestion box in city hall and invite the public to drop in their ideas for making the city a better place. Just think of the thousands of good ideas out there not being tapped.

What is the one thing you would never change?

I would always want to promote the cultural diversity of the city. Toronto is so unique. It is like the United Nations. I love it! When you travel a lot you learn to appreciate having "the world" in your own city.

What would your political enemies say about you?

They would probably say that I am too young and naive, too idealistic and unprepared for the responsibilities of being mayor. There would be the cynics who would question who is behind me or who is pushing me. Those individuals who believe that youth are not capable of anything but hanging around malls and playing video games.

Since every administration has at least one scandal, what would yours be?

I would let the street kids into the council chambers one night a year to have a pizza party.

How would you change the image of Toronto?

I think that it is really sad to see the number of people on the streets of Toronto, homeless and begging. This is a scandal in a rich country like Canada. I know that tourists find it hard to accept. We had a visitor from India who took pictures to "show the people back home." I would like people to think that we have enough compassion and resources to take care of our poor, our homeless and our children in trouble.

How would you improve Toronto's international reputation?

It should be easy. We are an international city. I would work more with the various ethnic groups and the contacts they already have in their countries. I would work with the school boards to twin schools in Toronto with others around the world, not only as a learning experience, but also so that young people can establish contacts and find ways in which they can contribute directly to the global community, especially in poor, developing countries.

What would be the biggest perk to being Mayor?

Having the opportunity to work with other people and to put our ideas in action. We all have our opinions on how we would like to improve our city. Having that opportunity would be the chance of a lifetime.

What lies would you tell to get elected?

I hope that when I reach the point when I start telling lies, I would have the courage and the common sense to quit.

What do you think would be the hardest part of the job?

Putting up with the critics who complain all the time but are never willing to find solutions.

What would you like historians to say about your reign as Mayor?

That I was able to break the stereotype that youth have nothing to contribute to society. I would like to have left the legacy of making Toronto a more humane place where all of its citizens were able to prosper.

TAKE ACTION! A Guide To Active Citizenship

Home	PART I	PART II
Preface, Contents	How To Get Involved: The Step-By-Step Process	The 'How To' Guide

Public Service Announcements

Another way to communicate with the public is through public service announcements (PSAs), which are messages about community events or important social issues broadcast on local radio and television stations. A public service announcement is a short commercial or advertisement. Most radio and television stations offer 10-, 20-, or 30-second spots for your message free of charge, as part of their broadcast licensing agreement with the government.

Here are some strategies to make the best use of your public service announcement:

- Contact your local stations and ask them about specific requirements before you write out your announcement. Do not forget about university and college radio and TV stations, including cable, as they are often an easy way to get your message out to the community.
- When you call the radio or TV station, ask to speak to the person who is in charge of public service announcements.
- Keep your PSA brief and to the point, as it is often easier to get shorter PSAs on the air.
- Start with radio messages first, as they are much easier to create and get broadcast. It is often very difficult to get a public service announcement on TV unless you can find someone who can professionally tape and edit your message. This can be very expensive. If you are uncertain about TV announcements or cannot find any help, stick with radio PSAs.

PART II > The How To Guide > How To Raise Public Awareness And Support

PART III
Where You Can Get Involved-
Everywhere!

PART IV
Tackling Social Issues

PART V
Sources And Resources,
End Notes

Format for a Public Service Announcement

Contact person:
Full name
Address
Telephone and fax numbers
Date

Necessary Information
- REGARDING: State what your PSA is about.
- TARGET AUDIENCE: Say which groups of people the PSA is hoping to inform (for example, young people, adults).
- AIRING DATES: State when your PSA should start and finish. You do not want your PSA on air after your event is over.

Message
- Make your PSA unique and interesting. Be youthful, but at the same time make certain that you grab the attention of the listeners. You may want to begin with a quick quote or a shocking statistic or fact.
- If your PSA is about an upcoming event, follow the 5Ws+H format (who, what, when, where, why and how).
- If your PSA is an advertisement to the public, be certain that you:
- state the name of your group.
- state the organization's mission or mandate (what your are trying to accomplish).
- provide some way listeners can get more information or contact you, such as referring them to your group's website, if you have one.

End Note
- Do not forget to write -30- at the end your PSA.
- Also indicate the length of time of the PSA in seconds below the message.

TAKE ACTION! A Guide To Active Citizenship

Home	PART I	PART II
Preface, Contents	How To Get Involved: The Step-By-Step Process	The 'How To' Guide

Sample Public Service Announcement

PUBLIC SERVICE ANNOUNCEMENT

Contact Person:
Calvin Michaels
864 Bluenose Street
Halifax, NS
Canada B3V 4T6
Tel: (902) 555-1234
Fax: (902) 555-2222
Cell: (902) 555-2323
cmichaels@hotmail.com

September 25, 20—

REGARDING: Teenagers Against Drunk Driving
TARGET AUDIENCE: Teenagers and young adults
AIRING DATES: Early fall (October 1 to November 30, 20—)

High school graduation is supposed to mark the beginning of a new period in the lives of young people, a time of hopes, dreams, and aspirations for the future. Tragically, all can be lost when someone gets behind the wheel of a car after drinking.

Teenagers Against Drunk Driving is a group of young people who are asking you to drive responsibly. Do not drive if you have been drinking. For more information about our group, please visit our website, located at www.teensagainstdrunkdriving.ca.

20 seconds

-30-

PART II > The How To Guide > How To Raise Funds

| **PART III** Where You Can Get Involved- Everywhere! | **PART IV** Tackling Social Issues | **PART V** Sources And Resources, End Notes |

HOW TO RAISE FUNDS

How to Put the *Fun* into Fundraising

Raising money to support your cause can be fun, rewarding, and a great way to publicize your cause. The money you raise can be used to fund the basic operating costs of your group, as well as projects that you decide to support.

There are hundreds of ways you can raise money, such as doing odd jobs, selling things, holding a fundraising event, writing proposals to receive grants, getting sponsors, and so on.

Odd Jobs

You and your group members can do odd jobs, such as

- Mow lawns: If possible, use human-powered mowers on small lawns. You will get a workout and you won't be creating air pollution.
- Rake leaves: Before getting out your rake, research, write, illustrate and sell tip sheets for turning raked leaves into fertile compost. This will give your leaf-raking added value and help to raise more funds. (Remember to print your tips sheets on 100 per cent recycled paper!)
- Shovel snow: Always remember to lift with your knees and whistle while you work! If you do not get snow where you live, be thankful! Shoveling snow is hard work.
- Plant and weed local vegetable, flower, and herb gardens: Before you knock on doors, research, write, and illustrate tip sheets on organic garden and lawn care. Sell these to add value to your gardening efforts.
- Walk dogs: Always pick up after dogs to show others you care about parks and green spaces.
- Baby-sit: Plan safe, fun activities to keep you and the children you baby-sit healthy and happy.

PART II > The How To Guide > How To Raise Funds

| **PART III** Where You Can Get Involved- Everywhere! | **PART IV** Tackling Social Issues | **PART V** Sources And Resources, End Notes |

Tip!

For safety reasons, inform your parents/guardians of your intentions before you perform any of these jobs, and only work for people that you know and trust.

Hold a Yard Sale

Are you ready to go through your closet and give away some of your used-but-still-useful toys, sporting goods, or clothes? Here are some strategies for holding a successful yard sale:

- The best time to hold a yard sale is in the spring, summer, or early fall when people are cleaning out their houses and are more likely to be outside.
- First make a list of the things you want to sell at your yard sale. When asking for donations, this list will be useful to give people an idea of the items you want most.
- Decide on a theme. For example, if your group is raising funds to support children's right to play, you might want to ask only for donations of sports equipment.
- Give your community plenty of time to lend a hand. You may want to advertise with flyers and posters.
- Look at the weather reports in advance and try to hold the yard sale when the weather is likely to be good.
- Ask your family members, including relatives, to donate items, even bigger things like pieces of furniture, to your yard sale.
- Ask your neighbors for donations as well, but make certain that you give them plenty of notice.
- To make the event fun for everyone, have other activities at your yard sale, such as children's games, face painting, and refreshments, which can help generate additional funding as well as content smiles. This way everyone will leave your yard sale feeling happy.

Host a Fundraising Event at Your School

Often, the best place to hold a fundraiser is at your school. Be certain to ask your principal or teacher advisor for permission before you start planning.

Here are 10 fun school fundraiser ideas:

1. **Movie night:** Rent a documentary movie that deals with your issue and invite the students in your school to watch. For this activity, you can't sell tickets, but your group can accept donations at the door. If you are really ambitious, ask a local media company to help you make your own movie and show this instead. You can provide popcorn and healthy snacks, donated by local businesses, with each donation.

2. **Greeting cards:** Sell funny, seasonal, or thought-provoking hand-made greeting cards to students, teachers, and parents. You can do this throughout the school year. This is a great fundraiser for people who like to write, draw, take pictures, or make crafts.

3. **Cooking classes:** Have local chefs donate their time to teach students and parents how to cook healthy and fun foods from around the world. Charge a price for the classes. Have the chefs go over and monitor kitchen safety.

4. **Eco-journals:** Make your own eco-journals from recycled paper, cardboard, used wrapping paper, and notebook binder rings. First do a survey, asking students what they like to see in a journal, and then get to work. Be as creative as you can, and sell your planet-friendly journals during lunch hour.

5. **School dances:** Organize a theme dance, like a 1970s disco dance, where people can dress-up in fun dance costumes. Have local actors or dancers donate their time to give groups of students dance lessons during the evening. This way, students will learn new dance moves while supporting your cause.

6. **Art show:** Organize an art show that features art pieces created from recycled materials. Your group can choose a theme to raise awareness, and either charge an admission fee, or sell the art pieces. This is a great way to involve your school's art classes, as well as local artists.

7. **Muffin Nations bake sale:** First, bake some wholesome and healthy muffins. Then, using vegetable-dyed icing, draw different United Nations country flags on the top of the muffins and sell them in your cafeteria to celebrate United Nations Day on October 24th. If it is a success, this can be a monthly or weekly event.

8. **Community picnic/dinner:** Have local businesses donate healthy food and beverages for a picnic-in-the-park event, and sell tickets to community members and families who want to enjoy some fun in the sun.

PART II > The How To Guide > How To Raise Funds

PART III
Where You Can Get Involved-
Everywhere!

PART IV
Tackling Social Issues

PART V
Sources And Resources,
End Notes

9. **Theater night:** Organize your school's gifted actors, class clowns, storytellers, and poets. Have them perform short skits, do stand-up comedy, share stories, and recite poetry. Advertise your event and charge an admission fee to raise money for your cause. Give donated prizes to audience members and participants.

10. **Water relay race:** Set up a water relay course at your school and have teams pay an entrance fee to compete. The trick is that water needs to be carried in a bucket balanced on each team member's head and cannot be spilled! Keep safety in mind when designing the course and involve your school's teachers and student's as cheering supporters. Give donated prizes to the teams who place first, second, and third.

Tip!

If you go out into your community, make certain that you travel in groups of two or three. It is a good idea to go with an adult as well, as you should never knock on a stranger's door alone.

SOUND BYTES:	OK!

  "**Don't be pushed by your problems. Be led by your dreams.**"

Anonymous

TAKE ACTION! A Guide To Active Citizenship

| **Home** Preface, Contents | **PART I** How To Get Involved: The Step-By-Step Process | **PART II** The 'How To' Guide |

The Budget

Before you begin fundraising, it is a good idea to create a budget that will provide you with information on how much money you will likely spend during your fundraiser and how much money you will collect after your event is over.

You may want to write up a budget that outlines your income (how much you will make) and your expenses (how much you will spend). Try to acquire as many donated items as possible. Ask local businesses if they would be willing to donate the materials you need. Tips for donated goods and services are provided in the next few pages.

A simple budget for a cooking class might look like the following:

PART III
Where You Can Get Involved-
Everywhere!

PART IV
Tackling Social Issues

PART V
Sources And Resources,
End Notes

Item	Income (how much you will make)	Expenses (how much you will spend)	Profit (your income less your expenses)
An estimated 20 parents will sign up for an evening cooking class and dinner at $20 per person	$400		
Selling of donated cookbooks to class participants: 15 cookbooks x $10	$150		
Services of cooking class instructor (local chef)		donated	
Groceries and cooking supplies from local grocery stores		donated	
Location of cooking class (school kitchen)		donated	
Biodegradable dish soap for after-class clean-up: 2 bottles x $5		$10	
Gift of appreciation purchased for cooking class instructor		$50	
TOTAL	*$550*	*$60*	*$490*

TAKE ACTiON! A Guide To Active Citizenship

Home	PART I	PART II
Preface, Contents	How To Get Involved: The Step-By-Step Process	The 'How To' Guide

Crazy Fundraisers Guaranteed to Work

1. Organize an indoor or outdoor sports tournament at your school. Charge teams an entry fee. Ensure each team has a teacher as a coach, the teams are fairly chosen, and the tournament is open to both boys and girls. Give donated prizes to the winning teams, as well as for the funniest mascot and the best team spirit.

2. Have a teacher agree to be weighed on a scale. Collect his or her weight in quarters. For example, if your teacher weighs 80 kilograms (176 pounds), collect the same weight in quarters. Collect donations of change from your peers, community members, and adult supporters.

3. Hold a school fashion show. Have local shops and community members donate cool and vintage clothing, hold your fashion show (ask teachers or students to model the clothes), and sell the clothes at the end of the event. Sell healthy refreshments and snacks to increase your event's success.

4. Hold a rock-a-thon. Get a group of students together who will stay up all night in your school's gymnasium rocking on rocking chairs. Before you start the event, collect pledges for every hour you spend rocking. Organize fun games and activities you can do at night while seated. Use your imagination.

5. Find a teacher or principal who would be willing to have his or her head shaved bald in front of the entire school if your group reaches its funding goal. Ask teachers with the most recognizable hairdos in school.

6. Organize a Taste of the Nations lunch or dinner. Set up tables representing various countries (put a flag on each table to identify the nation) and serve food from that region of the world (such as Indian, Italian, Greek, Japanese, or Mexican). Charge a fee for people to participate in the lunch or dinner event.

7. Hold a contest whereby participants pay a fee to try their luck at matching baby photos with your school's teachers. The person who gets the most correct answers wins a donated prize.

8. Invite a local radio station to host a student DJ contest at your school. Publicise the event throughout the school and accept donations at the door. Have the students vote on what student DJ they like the best and announce the winner over the radio and the school's PA system.

PART III
Where You Can Get Involved-
Everywhere!

PART IV
Tackling Social Issues

PART V
Sources And Resources,
End Notes

9. Ask permission from your teacher or principal to hold a school-wide contest whereby the lucky winner will receive one day free from homework. The contest idea is for you to decide. Charge a contest entry fee.
10. Host a talent auction. Ask skilled community members, carpenters for example, to donate their talents for one full Saturday or event and auction their services to the highest bidder. Winning bids will go to your cause. Remember to reward your skilled helpers with a thank-you dinner or with donated gifts.

Tip!

Ensure your event and prizes reflect the image of your organization. For example, if you are working to protect the environment, you may choose an environmentally-friendly product as a prize.

Ask the Community to Help

Obtaining community help is a great way to minimize the cost of your fundraising event. Ask for donated products and services that you can use as prizes, such as the following:
- Have a local photocopying business agree to copy your flyers onto recycled paper for free.
- A computer company might donate a computer for the use of your group.

101 FUNDRAISERS

IF YOU ARE LOOKING FOR MORE FUNDRAISING IDEAS, TAKE A LOOK AT THE FOLLOWING 101 FUNDRAISING SUGGESTIONS. THESE IDEAS ARE DESIGNED TO TRIGGER YOUR IMAGINATION. DO NOT FORGET TO THINK ABOUT SAFETY CONCERNS AS YOU MAKE YOUR PLANS, SUCH AS SEEKING PERMISSION WHERE NECESSARY, AND INFORMING PARENTS, GUARDIANS, AND TEACHERS OF YOUR PLANS. THE MOST IMPORTANT THING IS TO HAVE FUN.

1. JELLY BEAR COUNT: FILL A JAR WITH FRUIT JUICE BEARS AND HAVE PEOPLE PAY TO GUESS HOW MANY THERE ARE IN THE JAR. THE WINNER GETS THE JAR OF JELLY BEARS.

2. DRESS-DOWN DAY: IF YOU ATTEND A SCHOOL THAT REQUIRES A UNIFORM, HAVE A DAY IN WHICH ALL THE STUDENTS CAN WEAR CASUAL CLOTHES. ACCEPT A DONATION FROM EACH STUDENT WHO WANTS TO PARTICIPATE. MAKE CERTAIN THAT YOU ASK PERMISSION FROM YOUR PRINCIPAL FIRST.

3. BAND AND CHOIR CONCERTS: ASK YOUR SCHOOL BAND OR CHOIR TO DONATE THEIR TIME BY PERFORMING A BENEFIT CONCERT FOR YOUR CAUSE. INVITE YOUR COMMUNITY AND CHARGE ADMISSION FOR THE EVENT.

4. WALKATHON: CHOOSE A DATE AND A SCENIC AND SAFE WALKING ROUTE, MAKE UP SOME PLEDGE FORMS, AND ADVERTISE WITH POSTERS. HAVE EVERYONE WHO WANTS TO PARTICIPATE GATHER DONATIONS OR PLEDGES.

5. SELL GROCERY BAGS: ASK A LOCAL GROCERY STORE IF YOU CAN SELL REUSABLE ORGANIC COTTON BAGS AT THE CHECKOUT LINE. ACCEPT DONATIONS AS WELL, AND PUT UP A SIGN SAYING WHAT THE DONATION IS FOR.

- A trophy store might donate a trophy for your group to give to the winner of a contest.
- Local stores could donate prizes to be given away. Keep in mind some of these helpful hints when asking businesses for donations:
- Have a letter of introduction explaining to the business who you are and why you are asking for donations. Be sure to explain to the business how the donations will be used.
- Familiarize yourself with preparing a suitable proposal as some companies may specify the need for one before they can consider your request. See page 112 for tips on writing proposals.
- Whether you are writing a funding letter or a proposal, try to build a relationship with the business representative. Have the same person from your group communicate with the business. Have your parents/guardians suggest names of businesses to approach. Some will be businesses they know and deal with.
- Ask for donations early. Sometimes businesses have to get permission from an owner or a head office.
- Invite a representative from the business to your event and thank them publicly for the donation.
- Let people know which companies and individuals made donations by putting this information on posters and flyers. It is a nice way to say thank you.
- Once the fundraising project is complete, send out thank you letters and write a report outlining how much money the group generated. If a business makes a donation once, it is likely to make one again, but only if it feels its contribution was appreciated and sufficiently acknowledged. Keep a record of the business name, what it gave as a donation, to whom you spoke, and any other important facts you can remember.

SOUND BYTES: | OK!

"Learn from yesterday, live for today, hope for tomorrow.
The important thing is not to stop questioning."

Albert Einstein (1879-1955) Scientist

PART II > The How To Guide > How To Raise Funds

PART III
Where You Can Get Involved-
Everywhere!

PART IV
Tackling Social Issues

PART V
Sources And Resources,
End Notes

How to Write a Funding Letter

Writing a funding letter can be an easy way to let local businesses know about your group and how they can help by providing donated goods and services. In your funding letter, you will want to include the following:

- Information about your group and its mission.
- An explanation of the project or event that you are organizing.
- The type of donation you are seeking from the business.
- The type of recognition the business can expect to receive from you for the donation.
- Other donations you require. This is extremely important because the business representative may have contacts with other businesses that can provide the additional goods or services you need.
- A statement of thanks for their time and attention. Tell them that you look forward to hearing from them soon. Be sure to follow up no later than one week after the letter has been sent, either by visiting the business in person or making a phone call to the company.

101 FUNDRAISERS (CONT'D)

6. SKIP-A-THON: CHOOSE A DATE, MAKE UP PLEDGE FORMS, AND ADVERTISE WITH POSTERS. HAVE EVERYONE WHO WANTS TO PARTICIPATE GATHER DONATIONS OR PLEDGES, AND THEN SKIP YOUR WAY TO A HEALTHY HEART.

7. RAFFLES: SELL TICKETS AND KEEP THE TICKET STUBS. ON THE DAY OF THE DRAW, HAVE A PERSON CLOSE HIS OR HER EYES AND PICK A TICKET STUB FROM THOSE THAT WERE SOLD. DO THIS PUBLICLY. THE WINNER RECEIVES A DONATED PRIZE. MAKE SURE THE PRIZE IS SOMETHING PEOPLE WILL BOTH WANT AND USE.

8. KARAOKE NIGHT: ORGANIZE A FUN NIGHT OF KARAOKE SINGING. COLLECT DONATIONS AT THE DOOR AND SING YOUR HEART OUT. DRESS UP LIKE YOUR FAVORITE ROCK STAR TO ADD MORE FUN TO THE EVENT.

9. CALENDAR OF EVENTS: PUT YOUR CREATIVE SKILLS TO THE TEST AND CREATE CALENDARS TO SELL. ILLUSTRATE THEM AND ADD IMPORTANT LOCAL, NATIONAL, AND INTERNATIONAL DAYS. SELL THEM AT SCHOOL AND IN THE COMMUNITY.

10. COMMUNITY CARNIVAL: CHOOSE A SEASON AND HOLD A CARNIVAL IN YOUR LOCAL PARK OR SCHOOLYARD. INVITE STUDENTS, TEACHERS, AND THE COMMUNITY. CHARGE FOR ADMISSION OR A FEE TO PLAY FUN CARNIVAL GAMES.

11. PHOTOGRAPHY CONTEST: RAISE AWARENESS FOR YOUR ISSUE BY ORGANIZING A PHOTO CONTEST. ADVERTISE DIFFERENT CONTEST CATEGORIES AND CHARGE A SUBMISSION FEE. ASK A LOCAL BUSINESS TO DONATE PHOTO SUPPLIES, EVEN A CAMERA, AS PRIZES.

TAKE ACTION! A Guide To Active Citizenship

| **HOME** Preface, Contents | **PART I** How To Get Involved: The Step-By-Step Process | **PART II** The 'How To' Guide |

Sample Funding Letter

Jean Boulanger
863Lemay Avenue
Modesto, CA
78910 USA
(213) 555-2323

September 15, 20—

Ms. Elaine Silver
Juice Beverages Inc.
454 Rowanwood Blvd.
Modesto, CA
78910 USA

Dear Ms. Silver,

My name is Jean Boulanger. I am in the tenth grade at Greely High School. I work with an organization called Health for All. We are a youth organization whose mission is to help raise awareness of HIV/AIDS and donate money for research. As you may know, there were an estimated 2.8 million AIDS-related deaths in the year 2005 alone.

We are organizing a walkathon on October 15 to raise money for our group. We are seeking the support of Juice Beverages Inc. to donate 10 cases of juice as refreshments for the event. We would be happy to highlight the name and logo of Juice Beverages Inc. on all the promotional material that will be distributed for the event, as well as thank Juice Beverages Inc. publicly at the opening ceremonies of the walkathon.

We also require donated cups and food items. If you know of companies that might be interested in supporting our event, please get back to me. We hope to be able to raise $3,000 to donate toward HIV/AIDS research.

Thank you for your time and consideration. If you have any questions, please do not hesitate to contact me. I look forward to hearing from you.

Sincerely,
Jean Boulanger
Jean Boulanger

PART II > The How To Guide > How To Raise Funds

PART III
Where You Can Get Involved-
Everywhere!

PART IV
Tackling Social Issues

PART V
Sources And Resources,
End Notes

How to Write a Proposal

Proposals are another way to communicate your ideas and provide others with information on what you are trying to accomplish. When asking for donated materials, some companies ask for a proposal providing a full explanation about your group and how the donated goods will be used. On the following page is a basic outline on how to write a proposal:

101 FUNDRAISERS (CONT'D)

12. SPELLING BEE: LOOK THROUGH A TRUSTED DICTIONARY AND COME UP WITH A LIST OF WORDS OF INCREASING DIFFICULTY. HAVE PARTICIPANTS AND SPECTATORS PAY TO PARTICIPATE. THIS IS GREAT FOR PROMOTING LITERACY!

13. HOLIDAY CARDS: WORK WITH LOCAL BUSINESSES TO SELL HOLIDAY CARDS THAT YOU HAVE DESIGNED AND PRODUCED. BE SURE YOU CAN MAKE A LARGE ENOUGH PROFIT BEFORE PROCEEDING WITH THIS ACTIVITY.

14. BATTLE OF THE BANDS: GATHER TALENTED BANDS FROM YOUR LOCAL COMMUNITY. BOOK A VENUE AND ADVERTISE WITH POSTERS AND RADIO ANNOUNCEMENTS. HOLD A MINI-CONCERT AND LET THE AUDIENCE CHOOSE THE WINNING BAND.

15. PITCH-A-THON: RENT A RADAR GUN AND MEASURE HOW FAST PEOPLE CAN THROW A BASEBALL OR KICK A SOCCER BALL. CHARGE A FEE PER TRY AND GIVE A SPORTS-RELATED PRIZE TO THE FASTEST INDIVIDUAL.

16. SELL T-SHIRTS OR BUTTONS DISPLAYING YOUR LOGO: CREATE AN EYE-CATCHING AND CLEVER LOGO AND PRINT IT ON FAIR-TRADE T-SHIRTS AND BUTTONS. ADVERTISE AND SELL THE ITEMS FOR A REASONABLE PRICE.

17. CHILDREN'S PUPPET SHOW: MAKE PUPPETS WITH SOCKS AND CRAFT MATERIALS. PICK OUT OR WRITE A CHILDREN'S STORY. SET A DATE, TIME, AND LOCATION. ADVERTISE WITH POSTERS. SELL TICKETS IN ADVANCE AND AT THE DOOR.

18. MURAL ART: GATHER TOGETHER A GROUP OF CREATIVE YOUNG ARTISTS AND PAINT COLORFUL AND THOUGHT-PROVOKING MURALS IN YOUR COMMUNITY IN EXCHANGE FOR DONATIONS TO YOUR CAUSE.

TAKE ACTiON! A Guide To Active Citizenship

Home	PART I	PART II
Preface, Contents	How To Get Involved: The Step-By-Step Process	The 'How To' Guide

Format for a Proposal

Title
(Give your proposal a catchy title in the center of the
top of the page. Try to grab the attention of the reader).

- **To:** State the name of the address of the person or group to whom the proposal is being presented.

- **From:** State your name, full address, and phone and fax numbers.

- **Date:** Make certain that you write a date on your proposal

- Briefly explain the mission of your group. What are your trying to accomplish? It is a good idea to include the name of an adult supervisor, such as a teacher, in case the company wishes to contact another reference. Provide phone numbers or e-mail addresses for any reference(s) you list.

- State what it is that you want from the foundation or company.

- State how the foundation or company will be recognized for its donation.

- List the items required: Show the reader that you have done your homework and have thought about what you will need to put your plan into action. This is really important because the business representative may have contacts with other businesses that can provide the additional goods or services you require.

PART III
Where You Can Get Involved-
Everywhere!

PART IV
Tackling Social Issues

PART V
Sources And Resources,
End Notes

101 FUNDRAISERS (CONT'D)

19. HOST A THEME PARTY: DECIDE ON A FUN THEME RELATED TO YOUR CAUSE OF CHOICE. CHARGE AN ENTRANCE FEE, BUT BE SURE TO EXPLAIN TO PEOPLE THAT THEIR COVER CHARGE IS GOING TOWARD A GOOD CAUSE.

20. NEWSLETTER: CREATE A COLORFUL AND WELL-WRITTEN NEWSLETTER INFORMING YOUR PEERS AND COMMUNITY ABOUT YOUR ORGANIZATION AND CAUSE. SELL THE NEWSLETTER FOR A SMALL FEE. BE SURE TO LET PEOPLE KNOW HOW THEY CAN BECOME INVOLVED AND/OR DONATE TO YOUR CAUSE. HAVE SUPPLIES, LIKE 100 PER CENT RECYCLED PAPER, DONATED.

21. PLANT A TREE: ASK LOCAL NURSERIES FOR SEEDLING DONATIONS AND THEN HAVE COMMUNITY MEMBERS SPONSOR A TREE IN THE NAME OF A LOVED ONE OR PERSONAL HERO. PLANT TREES WITH YOUR COMMUNITY IN A PARK OR GREEN AREA.

22. GO THE DISTANCE: GATHER PLEDGES TO HAVE DANCE-A-THONS, ROCK-A-THONS, OR ANY OTHER TYPE OF ENDURANCE CONTEST YOU CAN THINK OF. ENCOURAGE PEOPLE TO WATCH AND CHEER YOU ON.

23. DAY OF COMMUNITY SERVICE: GATHER TOGETHER A GROUP OF FRIENDS, AND CONTACT A NUMBER OF LOCAL ORGANIZATIONS FOR WHICH YOU WOULD BE INTERESTED IN VOLUNTEERING. THEN HAVE PEOPLE SPONSOR YOU TO DO COMMUNITY SERVICE FOR 24 HOURS. YOU'LL BE HELPING YOUR COMMUNITY AND YOUR CAUSE!

24. FOOD FAST: GET TOGETHER WITH A GROUP OF FRIENDS, GATHER PLEDGES, AND FAST FOR A FULL 24 HOURS TO RAISE AWARENESS AND FUNDS FOR YOUR CAUSE. A GREAT WAY TO RAISE AWARENESS ABOUT HUNGER!

Sample Proposal

To: Mr. John Halford, Store Manager of The Gift Store
From: Christine Huang
          35 Oakridge Road
          Charlottetown, PEI
          Canada C2V 4X7

April 14, 20—

Our Group:

Teens Taking Action is a youth group based in Charlottetown dedicated to making the world a better place through community service projects and programs. Our mission is to help make our city a happier, more caring community. The teacher who serves as a mentor for our group is Mrs. Barton who can be reached by phone at (902) 555-6768, or by e-mail at barton@teenstakingaction.ca.

The Idea:

Teens Taking Action proposes a day of fun and community service. We would like to spend a day making gift baskets for senior citizens to show them that we care. This is important to us because we feel that senior citizens add a great deal to our community life. We think that this would be a nice way to say "thank you" for all of the guidance and support they have given to young people. The gift basket will be handed out at the Parkview Retirement Home.

The Request:

We would like The Gift Store to donate forty (40) medium-sized gift baskets, which we can fill with other donated products, as well as drawings and letters.

PART II > The How To Guide > How To Raise Funds

PART III
Where You Can Get Involved-
Everywhere!

PART IV
Tackling Social Issues

PART V
Sources And Resources,
End Notes

Recognition:

- Teens Taking Action would be more than happy to tell the recipients all about the generous donation from The Gift Store.
- The logo and address of The Gift Store will be highlighted on the Teens Taking Action website.
- Teens Taking Action will send out a press release about the project to local media and highlight the sponsorship of The Gift Store in the materials.

Other Requirements:

Teens Taking Action requires other materials to make this project a success. If you or your company know of any other business that we might approach to donate any of the following items, please let me know:

- hand cream, shampoo, and soap
- decks of playing cards
- fruit, cookies, and healthy snacks

Thank you for your time and consideration. If you have any questions, please do not hesitate to contact us. I look forward to hearing from you.

Sincerely,

Christine Huang
Christine Huang

101 FUNDRAISERS (CONT'D)

25. PIÑATA CONTEST: HAVE LOCAL BUSINESSES DONATE SMALL ITEMS AND HEALTHY TREATS TO PUT INTO A PIÑATA. CHARGE A FEE TO HAVE BLINDFOLDED PEOPLE TAKE TURNS TRYING TO BREAK YOUR HOMEMADE AND TREAT-FILLED PIÑATA.

26. CRAFT SALE: GATHER TOGETHER YOUR TALENTED FRIENDS AND LOCAL CRAFTSPEOPLE. HAVE THE CRAFTSPEOPLE DONATE TIME TO TEACH YOU HOW TO MAKE CRAFTS AND SELL THE CRAFTS AT YOUR LOCAL FARMER'S MARKET OR CRAFT SHOP.

27. PLANT A GARDEN: IN GREEN SPACES, ALONG SIDEWALKS, AND IN PLANTER BOXES, PLANT NATIVE FLOWERS AND PLANTS IN YOUR LOCAL NEIGHBORHOOD AND HAVE PEOPLE MAKE A DONATION FOR EVERY PLANT YOU PUT IN THE GROUND.

28. FAMILY BARBECUE: HOST A FAMILY BARBECUE FOR THE PEOPLE IN YOUR NEIGHBORHOOD. ACCEPT DONATIONS AT THE DOOR AND PREPARE INFORMATION SHEETS TO EDUCATE PEOPLE ABOUT YOUR ISSUE. HAVE FUN GAMES AND ACTIVITIES.

29. THREE-ON-THREE BASKETBALL TOURNAMENT: ORGANIZE A BASKETBALL TOURNAMENT IN YOUR SCHOOL WITH THE WINNING TEAM RECEIVING A DONATED PRIZE. THIS CAN ALSO BE DONE WITH SOCCER, BADMINTON, OR ANY OTHER SPORT.

30. SWIM-A-THON: GATHER ALL THE SWIMMERS YOU KNOW AND GET SPONSORS FOR THE NUMBER OF LAPS YOU SWIM. SET A DISTANCE GOAL AND USE A WELL-KNOWN BODY OF WATER FOR A BENCHMARK, SUCH AS SWIMMING LAKE ONTARIO! HAVE YOUR LOCAL POOL DONATE TIME AND LIFEGUARDS TO YOUR EVENT AND INVITE YOUR COMMUNITY TO CHEER YOU ON.

TAKE ACTION! A Guide To Active Citizenship

Home	PART I	PART II
Preface, Contents	How To Get Involved: The Step-By-Step Process	The 'How To' Guide

Grants and Foundations

A grant is a donation to be used for a specific group or project. To receive a grant, you have to submit a proposal to the group offering the grant.

Foundations are private groups that donate money to various causes. You often need charitable status from the federal government to receive money from foundations; however, there are some small community foundations that will give money to local causes and groups. You will have to write a proposal to the foundation if you hope to receive funding this way.

Large corporations sometimes give grants. You can make it a group project to contact a number of corporations. Ask someone in the public relations department of various corporations whether the company sponsors any grants.

Grants are often difficult to get, so do not expect them to be your main source of funding. However, it is worth trying because the amount of money you may receive can be quite large compared to the amount you would raise in a normal fundraising event.

Each foundation has its own requirements for grant proposals. Contact the program officer of the foundation to find out if your group is eligible for funding.

Tip!

Do not be discouraged if your proposal is not chosen. Ask for feedback from the company or foundation so that you might improve your next proposal.

SOUND BYTES:
OK!

"Only those who dare to fail greatly can ever achieve greatly."

Robert F. Kennedy (1925-1968) United States senator

PART III
Where You Can Get Involved-
Everywhere!

PART IV
Tackling Social Issues

PART V
Sources And Resources,
End Notes

101 FUNDRAISERS (CONT'D)

31. BEAT THE GOALIE: PICK THE BEST HOCKEY OR SOCCER GOALIE YOU KNOW AND INVITE PEOPLE TO TRY TO SCORE A GOAL FOR A PRIZE. EVERY PARTICIPANT HAS TO PAY TO PLAY.

32. BINGO: HOST A BINGO NIGHT AT A LOCAL COMMUNITY HALL OR SCHOOL. GIVE AWAY DONATED PRIZES.

33. NATIVE PLANT SALE: ORGANIZE A NATIVE PLANT SALE WITH PLANTS DONATED BY LOCAL NURSERIES AND CONSERVATION GROUPS.

34. GAMES NIGHT: ORGANIZE AN EVENING OF FUN BOARD GAMES.

35. BOAT RACE: ORGANIZE A MODEL BOAT RACE ON A BODY OF WATER. CHARGE A PARTICIPANT/SPECTATOR ENTRANCE FEE. THE WINNER OF THE RACE GETS A PRIZE. BE CAREFUL, THOUGH, TO WATCH OUT FOR DUCKS, TURTLES, AND FROGS!

36. FRESH FRUIT STAND: GET PERMISSION TO GO TO LOCAL FARMS AND PICK ORGANIC FRUIT TO SELL. SELL THE PRODUCE AT COMMUNITY MARKETS OR FESTIVALS. A GREAT WAY TO RAISE AWARENESS OF LOCAL FOOD ISSUES!

37. BOOK SALE: ASK YOUR FRIENDS, RELATIVES, AND TEACHERS TO DONATE THEIR OLD BOOKS. ADVERTISE YOUR BOOK SALE BY MEANS OF POSTERS AND FLYERS. SET UP A TABLE AND SELL THE BOOKS. SET ASIDE ONE QUARTER OF THE GOOD-QUALITY BOOKS AND DONATE THEM TO A NEEDY LIBRARY, SHELTER, OR SCHOOL.

38. BOWLING: ORGANIZE A TEAM BOWLING COMPETITION. CHARGE EVERYONE A SMALL FEE TO ENTER OR HAVE THEM GET BOWL-A-THON PLEDGES. ASK THE BOWLING ALLEY TO DONATE THE SPACE FOR YOUR EVENT.

TAKE ACTION! A Guide To Active Citizenship

| **Home**
Preface, Contents | **PART I**
How To Get Involved:
The Step-By-Step Process | **PART II**
The 'How To' Guide |

101 FUNDRAISERS (CONT'D)

39. BUY A BRICK: IF YOU ARE FUNDRAISING TO BUILD A SCHOOL OR BUILDING, HAVE PEOPLE MAKE DONATIONS TO PURCHASE BRICKS. BRICK BY BRICK, YOUR BUILDING WILL GROW BEFORE YOUR EYES!

40. ANIMAL BEHAVIOR: IF YOU LIVE IN AN AREA IN WHICH THERE ARE FARMS NEARBY, ORGANIZE A ONE-DAY FARM TOUR FOR CHILDREN AND THEIR PARENTS. TEACH THEM ABOUT LOCAL FARM ISSUES AND ANIMALS. CHARGE A FEE FOR YOUR TOUR.

41. COUPON SALE: HAVE COUPON BOOKS DONATED BY LOCAL RESTAURANTS, AND THEN SELL THEM TO STUDENTS AND ADULTS.

42. YOUTH COMICS: IN A GROUP, WRITE AND ILLUSTRATE CREATIVE, THOUGHT-PROVOKING, AND FUNNY COMICS THAT DEAL WITH YOUTH ISSUES. HAVE THE PRINTING SERVICES DONATED AND SELL THE COMICS AT YOUR SCHOOL.

43. BALLOON POP: BEFORE FILLING A BALLOON WITH AIR, PUT A NOTE INSIDE. HAVE A CERTAIN NUMBER OF THE NOTES WORTH A PRIZE. HAVE PEOPLE BUY BALLOONS AND POP THEM IN THE HOPE OF GETTING A PRIZE. BE SURE TO PICK UP THE BROKEN BALLOONS AFTERWARD.

44. SCAVENGER HUNT: SET A ROUTE AND MAKE A LIST OF ITEMS THE PARTICIPANTS NEED TO FIND IN ORDER TO WIN. ADVERTISE YOUR SCAVENGER HUNT AND CHARGE A FEE TO PARTICIPATE. THE WINNING PERSON OR GROUP GETS A PRIZE.

45. JEWELRY MAKING: FIRST, DO SOME RESEARCH. THEN, MAKE AND SELL YOUR DAZZLING JEWELRY.

PART II > The How To Guide > How To Raise Funds

| **PART III** Where You Can Get Involved- Everywhere! | **PART IV** Tackling Social Issues | **PART V** Sources And Resources, End Notes |

46. CAROL-SINGING: DURING THE CHRISTMAS SEASON, GO DOOR-TO-DOOR SINGING CAROLS FOR DONATIONS. HAVE A CARD WITH SOME BRIEF INFORMATION ABOUT YOUR ORGANIZATION TO GIVE TO SPONSORS. HAVE AN ADULT ACCOMPANY YOU. REMEMBER TO RESPECT THOSE WHO DO NOT CELEBRATE CHRISTMAS.

47. CANDLE-MAKING: HAVE A LOCAL CRAFTSPERSON SHOW YOU HOW TO MAKE BEESWAX CANDLES AND SELL THEM TO LOCAL SHOPS. THIS CAN BE EDUCATIONAL AND FUN, BUT BE SURE TO EXERCISE ALL HEALTH AND SAFETY PRECAUTIONS. MAKE SURE THE CANDLE WICKS ARE LEAD-FREE!

48. SPORTING EVENTS TICKETS: ASK SPORTS TEAMS TO DONATE SEATS FOR THEIR GAMES AND RAFFLE OFF THE TICKETS.

49 KNITTED GARMENTS: LEARN TO KNIT AND GET TO WORK MAKING NATURAL FIBER SOCKS, HATS, SCARVES—WHAT- EVER YOU WANT. DONATE A PORTION OF YOUR KNITTED GARMENTS TO A LOCAL SHELTER BEFORE SELLING YOUR FINISHED GOODS.

50. CHARITY BALL: HIRE A DJ OR A BAND, RENT A HALL, ADVERTISE, AND SELL TICKETS FOR A CHARITY DANCE.

51. CHRISTMAS ORNAMENT SALE: MAKE AND SELL HOME-MADE TREE ORNAMENTS DURING THE HOLIDAY SEASON.

52. CLASSIC CAR SHOW: ORGANIZE A CLASSIC AUTOMOBILE SHOW. INVITE PEOPLE TO ATTEND AS WELL AS TO BRING THEIR CARS BY PLACING ADS IN LOCAL NEWSPAPERS, LEAVING FLYERS AT LOCAL BUSINESSES, AND CHARGING PEOPLE TO COME AND SEE THE SHOW.

TAKE ACTION! A Guide To Active Citizenship

Home	PART I	PART II
Preface, Contents	How To Get Involved: The Step-By-Step Process	The 'How To' Guide

101 FUNDRAISERS (CONT'D)

53. MINIATURE GOLF: HAVE STUDENTS AND LOCAL CARPENTERS BUILD A SIMPLE BUT FUN MINIATURE GOLF COURSE AT YOUR SCHOOL, FEATURING RAMPS, WATER AND SAND TRAPS, AND OTHER OBSTACLES. CHARGE PEOPLE TO PLAY A ROUND.

54. LIFT-A-THON: HAVE SCHOOL ATHLETES LIFT WEIGHTS IN THE SCHOOL GYM AND COLLECT PLEDGES FOR EVERY KILOGRAM OR POUND THEY LIFT. MAKE SURE ALL PARTICIPANTS HAVE SPOTTERS TO ENSURE SAFETY.

55. SHORT STORY CONTEST: HAVE THREE LOCAL WRITERS ACT AS JUDGES, AND OPEN A SHORT STORY CONTEST FOR THE STUDENTS AT YOUR SCHOOL. PUBLISH THE WINNING ENTRY IN A LOCAL NEWSPAPER OR MAGAZINE AND AWARD DONATED PRIZES TO THE WINNING WRITERS.

56. MONOPOLY MATCH: HAVE A GROUP OF STUDENTS PAY A FEE TO ENTER A MONOPOLY TOURNAMENT WITH THE WINNER RECEIVING A DONATED BOARD GAME AS A PRIZE.

57. GUESS THE AGE OF YOUR TEACHER: ORGANIZE AN EVENT IN WHICH STUDENTS PAY TO GUESS THE AGE OF YOUR TEACHER. OBTAIN APPROVAL FROM YOUR TEACHER FIRST, OF COURSE.

58. HOOPLA: ORGANIZE AN EVENT WHERE COMPETITORS THROW HOOPS OVER DONATED PRIZES. THE PERSON WHOSE HOOP COMPLETELY LANDS OVER THE PRIZE GETS TO KEEP IT.

59. PUMPKIN-DECORATING CONTEST: AS HALLOWEEN APPROACHES, HOLD A PUMPKIN-DECORATING CONTEST AMONG DIFFERENT CLASSES IN EACH DIFFERENT GRADE. HAVE A TEACHER CARVE THE PUMPKIN AFTER THE CLASS HAS DESIGNED IT.

PART II > The How To Guide > How To Raise Funds

| **PART III** Where You Can Get Involved- Everywhere! | **PART IV** Tackling Social Issues | **PART V** Sources And Resources, End Notes |

60. DEBATE EVENING: RESEARCH A NUMBER OF ISSUES AND INVITE VARIOUS COMMUNITY MEMBERS TO DEBATE ISSUES. CHARGE THE AUDIENCE TO COME AND WATCH. THE ISSUES CAN BE FUN. FOR EXAMPLE, HAVE YOUR SCHOOL PRINCIPAL ARGUE THAT LISTENING TO MUSIC DURING CLASS ENHANCES A STUDENT'S ABILITY TO LEARN VERSUS A STUDENT WHO THINKS THAT MUSIC SHOULD BE BANNED FROM SCHOOL.

61. DOG SHOW: INVITE PEOPLE TO ENTER THEIR CANINE PETS IN A DOG SHOW. MAKE IT A COMPETITION THAT PEOPLE PAY TO ENTER, AND OFFER A PRIZE FOR THE BEST GROOMED DOG, BEST- AND LEAST-BEHAVED DOG, AND SO ON.

62. POPSICLE SALE: MAKE YOUR OWN POPSICLES FROM DONATED FRUIT JUICE AND SELL THEM ON A HOT DAY.

63. DUCK RACE: SELL NUMBERED NATURAL RUBBER DUCKS. SET ALL THE DUCKS AFLOAT IN A RIVER AND WATCH AS THEY RACE DOWNSTREAM TOWARD THE FINISH LINE. THE PERSON WHO BOUGHT THE DUCK THAT WINS THE RACE GETS A PRIZE.

64. SONG-WRITING CONTEST: OPEN A SONG-WRITING CONTEST IN YOUR SCHOOL AND HAVE LOCAL MUSICIANS ACT AS JUDGES. INVITE THE SCHOOL TO WITNESS THE SOLO PERFORMANCES AND CHARGE ADMISSION. GIVE MUSIC-RELATED DONATED PRIZES TO THE WINNERS.

65. COMEDY HOUR: HOST A COMEDY SKIT DURING LUNCH AT YOUR SCHOOL AND CHARGE PEOPLE TO ATTEND.

66. POPCORN PARTY: PLAN A MORNING TO MAKE POPCORN THAT CAN BE FLAVORED AND SOLD DURING LUNCH.

67. CHILDREN'S BOOK: WRITE AND ILLUSTRATE A CHILDREN'S BOOK TO SELL IN YOUR COMMUNITY. HAVE A LOCAL BUSINESS HELP YOU WITH THE DESIGN AND PRINTING OF YOUR BOOK.

68. FACE PAINTING: HAVE A FACE-PAINTING DAY. ADVERTISE IN ADVANCE AND THEN CHARGE A SMALL FEE FOR PAINTING YOUNG KIDS' FACES DURING A SCHOOL DAY OR ON A WEEKEND. CHOOSE A PLACE WHERE LOTS OF KIDS WILL BE.

69. CRAZY TIE CONTEST: HAVE STUDENTS COME TO SCHOOL WEARING THE MOST CREATIVE AND CRAZY TIE THEY CAN FIND. HAVE THEM VOTE ON THE CRAZIEST TIE WITH THE WINNER RECEIVING A PRIZE.

70. FLOWER SHOW: INVITE GARDENERS FROM YOUR COMMUNITY TO ENTER THEIR FLOWERS IN A COMPETITION FOR A DONATED GARDEN PRIZE. ASK VOLUNTEER EXPERTS TO BE JUDGES AND CHARGE PARTICIPANTS AND SPECTATORS A FEE.

71. HOW-TO VIDEO: CREATE A HOW-TO VIDEO, FOR EXAMPLE, OF HOW TO IMPROVE YOUR GOLF SWING, OR HOW TO MAKE CRAFTS. ASK LOCAL EXPERTS TO HELP YOU AND SELL THE FINAL PRODUCT.

72. FITNESS COMPETITION: ORGANIZE A FITNESS COMPETITION WITH A LOCAL FITNESS CLUB. ADVERTISE WELL AND CHARGE SPECTATORS TO COME AND WATCH PEOPLE COMPETE. YOU MAY NEED TO HAVE MEDICAL PERSONNEL ON HAND.

TAKE ACTION! A Guide To Active Citizenship

HOME	PART I	PART II
Preface, Contents	How To Get Involved: The Step-By-Step Process	The 'How To' Guide

101 FUNDRAISERS (CONT'D)

73. READ-A-THON: HAVE MEMBERS IN YOUR GROUP READ AS MANY BOOKS AS POSSIBLE IN A MONTH AND COLLECT NAMES OF SPONSORS WHO WILL DONATE A CERTAIN AMOUNT OF MONEY FOR EVERY BOOK READ.

74. "GET-OUT-OF-JAIL-FREE" CARD: HAVE STUDENTS PAY TO GET OUT OF A CLASS PERIOD FOR A DAY. ASK PERMISSION FROM YOUR TEACHERS OR PRINCIPAL FIRST. GIVE THEM A SPECIAL GET-OUT-OF-JAIL-FREE CARD TO SHOW THEY ARE PARTICIPANTS.

75. ART SALE: HAVE LOCAL ARTISTS DONATE SOME OF THEIR WORKS, OR ASK LOCAL BUSINESSES TO PURCHASE THEN DONATE ARTISTS' WORK, WHICH WILL BE DISPLAYED AND THEN SOLD TO THE PUBLIC.

76. GAME SHOW: RECREATE ONE OR MORE OF YOUR FAVORITE GAME SHOWS AND CHARGE CONTESTANTS A SMALL ENTRANCE FEE. SELL RAFFLE TICKETS TO THE AUDIENCE.

77. GARDENING: DO YOUR RESEARCH ON ORGANIC GARDENING METHODS AND THEN TEND THE GARDEN OF A NEIGHBOR, A LOCAL STORE, OR COMMUNITY PARK FOR A DONATION TO YOUR CAUSE.

78. GUEST SPEAKER: INVITE A GUEST SPEAKER WHO IS FAMILIAR WITH YOUR ISSUE AND SELL ADMISSION TICKETS TO RAISE FUNDS FOR YOUR CAUSE. GIVE THE SPEAKER A DONATED GIFT TO SAY THANK-YOU.

79. SCHOOL SUPPLIES STORE: SET UP A SCHOOL-RUN BUSINESS IN WHICH YOU SELL ENVIRONMENTALLY FRIENDLY SCHOOL SUPPLIES AND ART SUPPLIES TO SUPPORT YOUR CAUSE.

PART II > The How To Guide > How To Raise Funds

| **PART III** Where You Can Get Involved-Everywhere! | **PART IV** Tackling Social Issues | **PART V** Sources And Resources, End Notes |

80. **TOURIST VIDEO:** MAKE AND SELL A VIDEO FOR YOUTH TOURISTS OF PLACES TO GO AND COOL THINGS TO DO.

81. **KILOMETER/MILE OF COIN:** GATHER DONATIONS OF COINS (NICKELS, DIMES, OR QUARTERS; OR LOONIES AND TOONIES IN CANADA) AND LAY THEM SIDE BY SIDE UNTIL THEY STRETCH OUT TO BE A KILOMETER/MILE LONG (YOUR CHOICE). ALTERNATIVELY, SURROUND YOUR SCHOOL GYM, LIBRARY, OR PARKING LOT WITH COINS.

82. **RECIPE BOOK:** GATHER TOGETHER FAVORITE RECIPES AND PUT THEM TOGETHER IN A BOOK. SELL THE BOOK THROUGH YOUR SCHOOL, OR LOCAL COMMUNITY CENTER. ASK LOCAL BUSINESSES IF THEY WILL DONATE THE PHOTOCOPYING.

83. **MINI MARATHON:** HOLD A MINI MARATHON FOR STUDENTS AT YOUR SCHOOL AND HAVE PARTICIPANTS COLLECT PLEDGES FOR EVERY KILOMETER OR MILE THEY RUN. 10 KILOMETERS (5 MILES), OR MORE, THE DISTANCE IS YOUR CHOICE.

84. **TALENT SHOW COMPETITION:** INVITE PEOPLE TO SHOW OFF THEIR TALENT IN A COMPETITION IN WHICH THEY CAN WIN A PRIZE. SELL TICKETS IN ADVANCE.

85. **HENNA HAND-ART:** IF MEMBERS OF YOUR GROUP KNOW HOW TO APPLY HENNA (A TROPICAL PLANT USED AS A DYE), OFFER HENNA HAND-ART (ALSO CALLED MEHNDI) TO PEOPLE IN YOUR SCHOOL FOR A FEE.

86. **PET SITTING:** FOR A FEE, OFFER TO LOOK AFTER THE PETS OF YOUR FAMILY'S FRIENDS THEY ARE AWAY ON VACATION. MAKE SURE TO GIVE THEM LOTS OF LOVE AND EXERCISE.

TAKE ACTION! A Guide To Active Citizenship

HOME	PART I	PART II
Preface, Contents	How To Get Involved: The Step-By-Step Process	The 'How To' Guide

101 FUNDRAISERS (CONT'D)

87. TOY SALE: HOLD A TOY SALE JUST BEFORE CHRISTMAS. MAKE SURE THE TOYS ARE SAFE TO USE.

88. TRIATHLON: WITH THE HELP OF YOUR LOCAL RECREATION CENTER, SET A COURSE OF RUNNING, CYCLING, AND SWIMMING. HAVE PARTICIPANTS GET PLEDGES TO COMPETE TO WIN HEALTH-RELATED PRIZES.

89. LEMONADE STAND: MAKE LEMONADE FROM REAL LEMONS, AND SELL IT TO HOT AND THIRSTY PEDESTRIANS.

90. SNOW SCULPTURE CONTEST: GET STUDENTS TO ENTER A SNOW SCULPTURE CONTEST FOR A FEE. ASK LOCAL CELEBRITIES TO JUDGE THE SCULPTURES. IF YOU DON'T HAVE SNOW WHERE YOU LIVE, MAKE IT A SANDCASTLE CONTEST!

91. VALENTINE'S DAY DANCE: HOLD A SCHOOL DANCE FOR VALENTINE'S DAY AND DECORATE THE LOCATION IN RED AND WHITE. CHARGE AN ADMISSION FEE.

92. ST. PATRICK'S DAY PARTY: CELEBRATE ST. PATRICK'S DAY BY THROWING A PARTY AND GETTING EVERYONE TO DRESS UP IN GREEN, THE COLOR OF IRELAND!

93. SEED SALE: WHEN SPRING ARRIVES, SELL ORGANIC AND HERITAGE SEEDS TO GARDENERS IN YOUR COMMUNITY.

94. MOTHER'S DAY SALE: HAVE BUSINESSES DONATE ALL THE THINGS MOTHERS LOVE AND SELL THEM A DAY OR TWO BEFORE MOTHER'S DAY TO THE APPRECIATIVE FRIENDS, HUSBANDS, AND CHILDREN OF HARD-WORKING MOTHERS.

PART III Where You Can Get Involved- Everywhere!	**PART IV** Tackling Social Issues	**PART V** Sources And Resources, End Notes

A DAY ON THE WATER. CHARGE A FEE.

96. CANADA DAY (CANADA) AND INDEPENDENCE DAY (UNITED STATES) FESTIVITIES: ON THESE DAYS OF NATIONAL CELEBRATION, SELL REFRESHMENTS AND FOOD TO CELEBRATE THE OCCASION.

97. BACK-TO-SCHOOL DANCE: ORGANIZE A BACK-TO-SCHOOL DANCE TO REUNITE WITH OLD FRIENDS AND MAKE NEW ONES. CHOOSE A THEME AND DECORATE THE LOCATION. SELL TICKETS AND HAVE A BALL!

98. PUMPKIN SALE: AS HALLOWEEN FAST APPROACHES, ORGANIZE A PUMPKIN SALE. TO ADD VALUE, SELL STENCILS THAT PEOPLE CAN USE TO CARVE OUT INTERESTING DESIGNS ON THEIR PUMPKINS.

99. HALLOWEEN PARTY: HOLD A HALLOWEEN COSTUME PARTY IN YOUR SCHOOL GYMNASIUM. DEVOTE A CORNER OF THE GYM TO A HAUNTED HOUSE. SELL TICKETS TO THE PARTY AND ACCEPT DONATIONS TO YOUR CAUSE AT THE ENTRANCE TO THE HAUNTED HOUSE.

100. CANADIAN AND AMERICAN THANKSGIVING TURKEY RAFFLE SALE: ASK LOCAL TURKEY FARMERS TO DONATE SEVERAL ORGANIC, FREE-RANGE TURKEYS TO BE RAFFLED OFF. APPROACH FARMS WHERE THE TURKEYS ARE TREATED TO A HEALTHY DIET, HAVE ROOM TO ROAM, AND ARE TREATED ETHICALLY.

101. CHRISTMAS TREE SALE: AS THE HOLIDAY SEASON BEGINS, MARKET AND SELL CHRISTMAS TREES IN YOUR COMMUNITY. ASK LOCAL GROWERS TO DONATE THE TREES OR HAVE BUSINESSES SPONSOR THE EVENT. IF POSSIBLE, GET YOUR TREES FROM GROWERS WHO USE ORGANIC AND ENVIRONMENTALLY SUSTAINABLE METHODS TO GROW THE TREES.

PART III Where You Can Get Involved- Everywhere!	**PART IV** Tackling Social Issues	**PART V** Sources And Resources, End Notes

Being committed to positive change doesn't mean you have to take on the whole world. You can get involved wherever you find the need for change or the opportunity to help others. Look around you. Do you see anything at school, around your home, or in your community that could be helped or improved? Challenge yourself to think creatively and constructively about the world. Develop concrete ways to make it a more positive place. Remember that you have both a right and a responsibility to help find solutions to problems that touch your life and the lives of your peers. There are many ways that you can make a difference, and your every contribution counts.

SOUND BYTES: OK!

> ⚠ *"What you do may seem terribly insignificant, but it is terribly important that you do it anyway."*
>
> *Mahatma Gandhi (1869-1948) Leader, Indian national movement*

AT HOME

Your actions to make the world a better place can begin in your own home. It is important that you respect and show concern for the quality of life of others. Whatever your family arrangements, you can help out with some of the work that needs to be done on a daily basis. The people with whom you live will be grateful because your contributions will be making a difference to your home environment.

TAKE ACTION! A Guide To Active Citizenship

HOME	PART I	PART II
Preface, Contents	How To Get Involved: The Step-By-Step Process	The 'How To' Guide

Here are a few ways to help out around your home:

* Help clear the table after meals.
* Do the dishes.
* Try doing the vacuuming.
* Help younger brothers and sisters with their homework.
* Baby-sit.
* Take care of your pets. Feed them regularly, and make sure that they always have fresh water, exercise, and plenty of love.

PART III > Where You Can Get Involved > At Home

PART III
Where You Can Get Involved-
Everywhere!

PART IV
Tackling Social Issues

PART V
Sources And Resources,
End Notes

* Return library books for other family members.
* Shovel snow or clear ice.
* Help with the laundry.
* Try to help members of your family who do not live with you, such as your grandparents, aunts, uncles, and cousins. They may appreciate a visit as much as anything, but remember to arrange it ahead of time.

You can probably think of many more ways to make a positive contribution to your home. Make a list and start surprising your family.

Plan a Family Togetherness Activity

Households can be very busy and even hectic. With each member of the family involved in his or her own activities, it can be difficult to find time to spend together. Taking some time to enjoy one another's company can help keep a family feeling connected.

Choose an idea

Talk to your family members, or the other people with whom you live. How much time does everyone have? A day? An evening? Will you stay in or go out? Determine the types of activities that every family member prefers and then choose to do something that appeals to everyone. Some fun ideas that a lot of people enjoy are:
* a pizza and movie night
* going on a picnic
* going for a walk or hike

There are lots of other things you can do. Be creative and open to suggestions. The most important thing is that you all have fun together. With any activity, planning is an important part of the process.

Choose a date

Once again, talk to everyone involved to determine some possible dates and times for your activity. Choose a date when everyone is free and plan it well in advance so that everybody can participate.

Decide who will participate

You may want to include other people in your Togetherness Activity, such as grandparents or cousins. All family members should make this decision together.

Do not forget!

Leave reminders for everyone. Make colorful notes and post them on the refrigerator, on a house bulletin board, or on bedroom doors.

Enjoy your activity

Enjoy one another's company. Thank everyone for participating, and gather ideas for the next activity.

Tip!

If you are including people who do not live in your home, think of a way to remind them about the activity. You might phone or e-mail them, or mail them a note.

PART III Where You Can Get Involved- Everywhere!	**PART IV** Tackling Social Issues	**PART V** Sources And Resources, End Notes

AT SCHOOL

The possibilities for involvement at school are endless. Your school is filled with amazing people who have various talents and interests. Getting together and getting involved will lead to a lot of new friendships. Always speak with a teacher or to your principal to get permission before you start any projects, and try to get them involved as well.

Here are some ideas to get you started:

- Be a friend to new students at your school. Show them around and introduce them to your friends and teachers. By being a friend, you will gain a friend yourself and you will also improve your communication and interpersonal skills.
- Help out with younger classes. Young children admire older students. You can do fun and educational activities, such as reading, drawing, or painting.
- Help younger students do their homework and develop your presentation and communication skills at the same time.
- Organize a fundraising event to finance school activities. In the process, you will develop your organizational skills and inspire others through teamwork.
- Encourage school spirit by organizing an activity of the month, such as school dances, fashion shows, sporting events, or games. Discover how you too can work with the media and inform people about fun activities.
- Become a student representative. If your school does not have a student government, talk to a teacher or your principal about starting one. You will become a better public speaker in the process.
- Become a journalist for your school newspaper, or a disc jockey for your school radio station. If your school does not have a newspaper or radio station, talk to your teacher or principal about starting one. Such great activities help you to become a critical thinker, proficient writer, and a better researcher.
- Work as a peer tutor, counselor, or mentor. You can participate in conflict mediation, helping to settle disputes in a fair way, or listen when fellow students need someone to talk to. You will need training to do these things. Does your school offer any of these programs? If not, you may want to talk to your guidance counselor or principal about the idea. By doing so, you will become a great listener and perhaps a close friend.

- Promote after-school safety. Raise awareness among students about crosswalkand school bus safety, as well as home safety. Presenting a plan of action to implement the after-school safety program will give you valuable experience with running an effective meeting.

Encourage School Spirit with Spirit Week

Spirit Week is intended to get people involved in school activities and to be proud of their school. Encourage everybody to participate. Try to come up with activities that appeal to a variety of interests. This will help you draw out different groups of students from all over your school, and get them excited about getting involved.

Choose an issue

Decide what you want to accomplish with Spirit Week and the best way to go about it. Is there a specific message you want to get across to your classmates, or a theme that you know would unite them? Think of what your whole school could accomplish once Spirit Week has inspired and motivated every student. In what direction could you focus all that positive energy to do something productive as a team?

Do your research

Ask your teacher or principal to get involved in a Spirit Week. Request their advice, and that of your student government leaders for advice on how to organize one. Discuss possible dates with your principal and student leaders. Make sure the date you choose will not conflict with other activities that are already planned, such as a career week or a sports tournament.

Build a team

You can accomplish a lot on your own, but it will require the efforts of a team to make Spirit Week happen. The more people who are involved in planning, the more ideas there will be. The workload can be divided among the team members so no one person is overwhelmed with tasks.

PART III
Where You Can Get Involved-
Everywhere!

PART IV
Tackling Social Issues

PART V
Sources And Resources,
End Notes

Call a meeting

Speak to your friends and classmates and let them know about Spirit Week. Encourage them to get involved and to help you develop a plan of action. You may also want to solicit some input from teachers and your principal. Set a date to gather your team members to discuss the issues.

Make a plan of action

Here are a few items you will need to discuss:

- What will be the theme or main events of Spirit Week? For example, you might have everyone dress up according to a different theme on each day of Spirit Week: Pajama Day, Backwards Day, Inside-Out Day, Wacky-Tacky-Tie Day, Hawaiian-shirt Day, just to name a few. Alternatively, encourage all the clubs and organizations in the school to do something to show people what they are about. You can hold a general assembly with speeches, music, and school chants. If you have a school band, they may want to play at the assembly. You could even invite local celebrities to attend.
- Are you planning to reach out into the community? While everyone is in the spirit, try to think of ways you can use Spirit Week to show your community that the students in your school care. For example, you could hold a food drive as part of Spirit Week and arrange to deliver the goods you collect to the food bank.
- How will you advertise Spirit Week? Advertise your event by making large, colorful posters and flyers. Put an announcement in the school newspaper. Remind people about Spirit Week over your school's public announcement system (with permission, of course). Try other ways you can think of to let people know about your event.

Take action and then review

There will be a lot of coordinating to do during Spirit Week, but if there are plenty of volunteers, it will be lots of fun. Enjoy all of the activities.

At the end of Spirit Week, bring your team together and talk about the good points of the event, as well as some lessons that were learned in order to make other Spirit Weeks even better. You may want to create a checklist to use for your next Spirit Week.

Have fun!

Have fun while organizing Spirit Week and enjoy strengthening the spirit and energy of your school. After your event has been successfully completed, hold a celebration or host a party to thank all of your team members.

Take Action to Give Students Power

Becoming involved at school can give you and your fellow students a voice and power in issues that concern you. Here are some ideas for such projects:

- Involve the student body in writing a constitution for the student government.
- Involve the student body in writing a charter of student rights and responsibilities.
- Take action to have a student representative on the local school board and the parent-teacher association or school council.
- Work with your local government representative to set up a youth council for your community, your province, or your country.
- Petition for an ombudsperson for children at all levels of government.

Start a Club With a Purpose

Starting a club with a purpose is a great way of gathering a group of students who share a common passion, and directing their joint energy towards a specific goal. When group members choose a collective goal and focus all of their unique strengths towards it, there is no limit to what can be accomplished. A club with a purpose not only cultivates passion and energy around a shared cause, it helps everyone involved think creatively and purposefully about the things they care about.

Environmental Club

- Clean up your environment at school. You and your friends can pick up litter on school grounds and cover up graffiti. Get permission from a teacher first, and never touch any broken glass or needles. Promote recycling. Get permission to start a garden or a compost pile behind the school building.
- Organize a garbage-free lunch. Encourage students to store food in reusable containers and to pack lunches in reusable organic cotton bags. Encourage everyone to make garbage-free lunches an everyday habit and the amount of garbage in landfills will decline dramatically.

PART III Where You Can Get Involved- Everywhere!	**PART IV** Tackling Social Issues	**PART V** Sources And Resources, End Notes

Helping Hands Club

* Decide who is in need in your community and then organize events that will benefit them. For example, organize a toy sale. Use the profits you make to buy new environmentally-friendly toys for children in need, or to buy gifts for residents in senior citizen homes.
* Organize an organic and healthy food drive to aid a local food bank.

Debating Club

- Choose topics from current events, and have people represent different sides of an issue. Try representing the side you do not agree with. You will educate yourself about important issues and learn to understand other people's points of view.

Human Rights Club

- You and your friends can join organizations that are concerned with human rights (see Part 5 for contact information).
- Have individual members research various human rights issues, and then convene the group to share the results.
- Hold fundraising events to support your cause.
- Invite guest speakers to your school. (You will need to involve the principal in this endeavor.) Guest speakers could include such people as city councilors, members of Parliament (in Canada), members of Congress (in the United States), experts in various fields, or anyone who you think has an interesting message.

IN YOUR COMMUNITY

There are many ways to get involved in your community. Keep your eyes open when you are riding your bike or walking around the area where you live. Is there a food bank? Are there any seniors' residences? Is there a park for children? Is there graffiti on the walls of the neighborhood buildings? Are there trees? Are the streets clean?

A real community values every member for his or her contribution. People work together to make the community a good place for everyone.

There are plenty of things you can do to make a difference in your community.

PART III Where You Can Get Involved- Everywhere!	**PART IV** Tackling Social Issues	**PART V** Sources And Resources, End Notes

SOUND BYTES: OK!

> "To accomplish great things we must not only act, but also dream; not only plan, but also believe!"
>
> *Anatole France (1844-1924) Writer and critic*

Here are a few suggestions:

- Organize a neighborhood barbecue or a community garage sale for charity. Encourage everybody to come out and get to know the neighbors.
- Create a neighborhood watch system for kids, or introduce a Block Parents program.
- Get involved in land preservation. Is there a piece of land in your area that you think should stay as green space? Write letters and petitions to try to prevent developers from building on it.
- Help elderly neighbors with chores, such as shopping for groceries, mowing lawns, pulling weeds, or shoveling snow. They will appreciate the help, and will also enjoy your company.
- Start a neighborhood beautification program. Involve other young people in this project; it is more fun when you work together. Paint fences and clean up graffiti. Pick up litter in vacant lots, playgrounds and parks, and around streams and lakes. Always get permission from an adult, and be very careful. Never touch any broken glass, needles, or condoms.

After a day of helping out in your community, gather your team together and have some fun to celebrate the contributions you have made. When you end the day feeling great about your work, you and your friends will be inspired to continue making a difference.

TAKe ACtiON! A Guide To Active Citizenship

| **Home**
Preface, Contents | **PART I**
How To Get Involved:
The Step-By-Step Process | **PART II**
The 'How To' Guide |

Organize a Drive

Holding a drive can draw together an entire community. When you organize a drive for food, clothes, or other important supplies, you make those who are more fortunate aware of the problems within their community, and provide them with a way to take part in a concrete solution. At the same time, you are helping the less fortunate understand that they are not alone and that their community is working to help improve their lives. A drive can teach the organizers, participants, and the people in need that every small contribution makes a difference.

Choose an issue

Organizing a drive is a great way to serve your community. You might find yourself in need at some point in your life, so it is your duty as a citizen to do what you can to assist those who are hungry, homeless, or impoverished. When you support services such as food banks and shelters for the homeless, you are demonstrating to the people who use them that their community cares.

SOUND BYTES:　　　　　　　　　　　　　　　　OK!

"We live surrounded by a sea of poverty. Nevertheless, this sea can decrease in size. Our work is only a drop in the bucket, but this drop is necessary."

Mother Teresa (1910-1997) Catholic nun, humanitarian

PART III > Where You Can Get Involved > In Your Community

| **PART III** Where You Can Get Involved- Everywhere! | **PART IV** Tackling Social Issues | **PART V** Sources And Resources, End Notes |

Do your research

- Ask officials at community food banks or shelters if they would like you to hold a drive. If so, determine what their greatest area of need is; for example, winter clothing, canned food items, shoes, sleeping bags, and so on.
- Find out how you can organize such a drive. Involve an adult sponsor if you need one. Choose a school or community event that you can take advantage of, and request permission from the organizers to piggyback your drive on their event. For example, if you want to hold the drive in conjunction with a school concert, ask the principal to become involved.

Build a team

Tell your friends and neighbors about the drive and determine how they can help. There are many things that need to come together in order to organize a successful drive.

Call a meeting

Speak to your team and seek their advice on how to proceed. Assign roles and responsibilities.

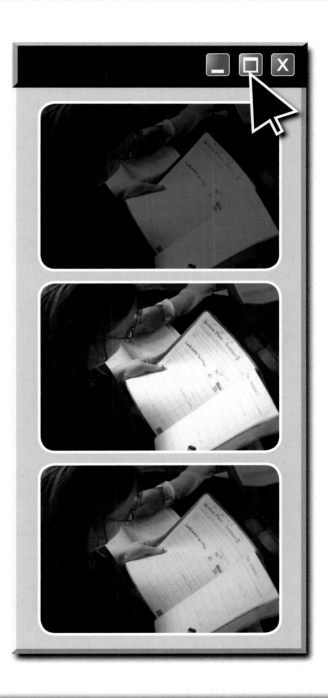

TAKe ACtiON! A Guide To Active Citizenship

| **Home** Preface, Contents | **PART I** How To Get Involved: The Step-By-Step Process | **PART II** The 'How To' Guide |

Make a plan of action

Here are a few things you will need to decide:

- How will you let people know about your drive? You could, for example, advertise your food drive in the school and in the community. If the drive is part of a special event, let people know that the event and drive are happening at the same time so they will remember to bring items for your drive. One idea is to have a donated item serve as admission for the event, such as for a dance or movie night.
- Make eye-catching flyers and posters. Send an announcement to the local newspaper. Inform the student body during morning announcements. Can you think of other ways to let people know about the event and your special drive?
- How will you hold the donations: in large boxes, bins, or baskets?
- Where will you put the bins?
- How will you transport the donations to the food bank after the event?
- What other logistical requirements do you need to work out?

Take action and then review

Follow through with all of your actions and have a back-up plan in place, just in case. Do not leave anything to chance. If the boxes fill up, make sure there are always others handy for more donations.

Donate the goods. Bring the food, clothes, shoes, and other items that you have received to the food bank or shelter.

Thank all organizers of the event for their co-operation in making the drive a success. Also thank the people who made donations and encourage them to donate to the shelter or food bank throughout the year.

Soon after the drive, bring your team together and share what was good about the event, as well as any lessons that were learned so that future drives can be better planned and executed.

Have fun!

Have fun organizing the drive and take pride in knowing that you are helping to relieve the suffering of people in your community.

PART III > Where You Can Get Involved > In Your Community

| **PART III** Where You Can Get Involved- Everywhere! | **PART IV** Tackling Social Issues | **PART V** Sources And Resources, End Notes |

SOUND BYTES: OK!

> "You miss 100 per cent of the shots you never take."
>
> *Wayne Gretzky (b.1961) Coach and former NHL hockey star*

Rally or a Forum

When you organize a rally or a forum, you are creating a space for people to communicate their ideas freely and share their visions for positive change. When people are given the opportunity to express their knowledge and feelings about a cause, their passion can inspire and motivate an entire crowd to take action. You can organize a rally or a forum relating to a particular cause or theme important to your community and invite speakers to relay their thoughts, personal experiences, and messages to the public.

Points to Consider:

1. What jobs have to be done?
* In preparation for the event?
* During the event?
* After the event?

2. **Location**
* What is a good location?
* Is it the right size? (Not too big, but not too small.)
* Is the location accessible by public transportation?
* Are washroom facilities available?
* What is the cost? Is a permit necessary?

TAKE ACTION! A Guide To Active Citizenship

Home	PART I	PART II
Preface, Contents	How To Get Involved: The Step-By-Step Process	The 'How To' Guide

3. **Responsibilities:**
* Who will be the key person in charge?
* Who can we ask to speak at the event?
* Are there important individuals you can ask to participate? Who will contact these individuals? Who will meet/invite the speakers?
* Who will be the master of ceremonies?
* Will there be music at the event? Who will organize it?
* Who will be responsible for advertising the event?
* What equipment is necessary?
* How will the event be advertised?
* Who will prepare the press release?
* Who will handle the press?
* Who will be responsible for cleaning up?
* Who will send thank you letters?

4. **Logistics/Money**
* How will we raise the money to sponsor the event?
* Who can we ask to contribute donations to the event?
* Who will be responsible for finances?
* Will we have a display at the event? A sign?
* Who will set up the display? Who will make the sign?
* Who will distribute literature at the event?
* At what time will the organizers meet?
* At what time will the event begin?

Now that you have asked yourself all of these questions, do not get discouraged. Rallies or forums can be a great success if done well. Begin to delegate to your team members various areas of responsibility and encourage them to exercise their leadership capabilities. It is also recommended that you find an adult who is familiar with organizing such events to serve as a mentor for you and your team.

PART III > Where You Can Get Involved > In Your Community

| **PART III** Where You Can Get Involved- Everywhere! | **PART IV** Tackling Social Issues | **PART V** Sources And Resources, End Notes |

More Actions to Take to Get Your Message Across

Once you have educated yourself on an issue, you have both a right and a responsibility to share your knowledge and passion with the people around you. When your community sees how strongly you feel about your cause, they may be inspired and motivated to join your campaign. Be creative when you are trying to get your point across. People will remember what you have said if you can phrase your message in a unique and exciting way.

Street Theatre

One of the most popular means of educating the public in the developing world is through street theatre. Groups perform skits, sing, read stories, recite poetry, or use puppets to create awareness of issues affecting youth. You may want to try these ideas in a public place—for example, at your school or at a rally. Depending on the location you choose, you may have to obtain permission first.

March

March or walk down the street, to your school, to city hall, or across the park. Marches or walks may be used simply to educate the public or to raise funds for your cause. If you are planning a large march, it is recommended that you contact the police ahead of time to inform them of your plans and to inquire if there are any laws, restrictions, or permits required. Make sure that parents/guardians or teachers are aware of your intentions.

Organize carefully where your group will march and how you will publicize the event. Set up a telephone tree to invite as many young people as possible to participate in your march. Have a sign-in table to take the names of the participants for future activities. You may want to carry signs to deliver a message to the public. You may also consider using walkie-talkies or cell phones so that the leaders in the front and back of the line can communicate.

TAKE ACTION! A Guide To Active Citizenship

| **Home**
Preface, Contents | **PART I**
How To Get Involved:
The Step-By-Step Process | **PART II**
The 'How To' Guide |

PART III > Where You Can Get Involved > Working With Government

| **PART III** Where You Can Get Involved- Everywhere! | **PART IV** Tackling Social Issues | **PART V** Sources And Resources, End Notes |

WORKING WITH GOVERNMENT

An important part of being socially active is being aware of your role as a citizen and your relationship with your government. This means understanding the problems and concerns of your community and how the policies of your government affect your community. As an active citizen, you must learn how to participate within your community and how to influence the government directly and effectively. When you stand up to have a say in your government, you are asserting your power to effect positive change.

1. Be prepared

Getting involved in social issues can sometimes lead to working with governments and government officials. Governments exist to serve the people they represent, so do not be afraid to speak out about issues that concern you. This is a big step. Be prepared. Do your research. Make sure that you understand the issue.

Since governments represent all of the people in a given area, you may have to demonstrate that a lot of people agree with you before the government will act on your suggestions. Part 2 examines in more detail some strategies you can use—such as surveys, petitions, and the media—to demonstrate that you have the support of many people.

2. Do not be afraid to attend public meetings and express your opinion

Your community may hold a meeting to discuss a bill or a community proposal (for example, close a library, turn a park into a parking lot, plant trees, etc.). This would be a great opportunity to express your opinion and have it on record. Others may be influenced by your words. Testifying as a witness is very much like making a speech. Refer to the section "Public Speaking," beginning on page 59 in Part 2, for some helpful tips.

3. Do not be afraid of criticism

Naturally, people's opinions on various issues differ. Some people may not agree with you, but do not be discouraged if this happens. Focus on your issue, and do not take any difference of opinion personally. Instead, try to learn from criticism you receive; it will make you and your work stronger.

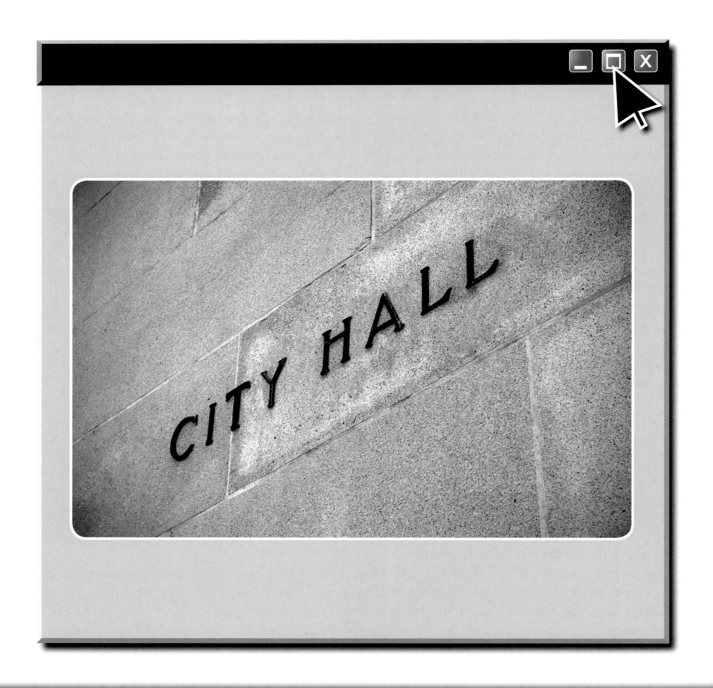

Working with governments often involves influencing people and trying to convince them about the merit of your point of view. The more you know about your issue, the more effective your arguments will be and the more confident you will become.

Tip!

Influencing your government is serious business and it is quite natural to feel nervous about getting involved with government officials. But do not forget that you are a citizen and that your opinion counts. Take strength from the many other young people who have been in this same position and probably felt as you do now. Ask an adult or a friend to help you, if necessary.

Influencing Your Local Government

Your local government has jurisdiction over police, fire and ambulance services, parks, street cleaning, zoning by-laws, and public transit. Government decisions in these areas can affect you directly, and so there is a natural tendency to become most passionate about these types of issues. Rallying people to a local cause and appealing to your local government has great potential for success and can result in changes that influence the daily life of your community.

Contact an elected official

Contact the elected official in your area and ask for his or her support. For instance, you may need help starting a youth council in your community, where young people would have a voice on issues that concern them. Or, you may want an elected official to draft and introduce a bill to support a particular cause. When you meet the official, be well prepared with facts and other information about your issue. Elected officials represent the people, but they are very busy; you need to get their attention and make your point quickly and strongly. Convincing them to work with you is the first step.

Let people know

Promote your cause by using the media and getting support from the community. Media coverage of an issue will help to influence the government. Create colorful posters and flyers and obtain permission, if necessary, to post them in high-traffic areas, such as the public library, the community center, and schools. You may also want to write a letter to the editor of your local newspaper. Try to think of other ways you can get your message across to the greatest number of people. (Part 2 contains some additional ideas.) Be sure to provide an address where people can get in touch with you or your group for more information or to volunteer to help. The more people involved in your cause, the greater your chance of influencing your local government's position on an issue.

Organize a petition

Write a petition supporting the bill your elected official will be introducing on your behalf. This will help the official prove that there is plenty of community support for your idea, which will increase the chance of the bill becoming a law. Your petition should state the issue, say why it is important, and ask for the bill to be passed. Refer to the section "Making a Petition" beginning on page 73 in Part 2 for more specific instructions. Get as many signatures as you can, and then submit the petition to your elected official.

Other Ways to Get Involved with Government

There are many ways of getting involved with your government. You can research the structure of your government, become a student representative on a community youth council, or volunteer in a campaign or on a council. These are all challenging and exciting ways of helping you understand how government words. Remember, knowledge is power. Once you have learned the system, you will have the power to influence the decisions it makes.

Learn about your system of government

In Canada, you could:

- Visit your provincial legislature or your nation's capital to learn about the federal government.
- Write to the House of Commons requesting information about how the government works.
- Be familiar with Canada's Constitution. Your local library should have a copy of this document.

TAKE ACTiON! A Guide To Active Citizenship

Home	PART I	PART II
Preface, Contents	How To Get Involved: The Step-By-Step Process	The 'How To' Guide

In the United States, you could:

- Visit your state legislature or your nation's capital to learn about the federal government.
- Write to Congress requesting information about how the government works.
- Be familiar with the United States Constitution. Your local library should have a copy of this document.

Become a student representative

- If your school does not have a student government, start one.
- Urge your parent-teacher association (PTA) or student council to create a student representative position within the association.
- Get involved in other organizations that might need and welcome a youth perspective.

Volunteer at your city councilor's office

All of these activities will give you experience that will help you to understand how governments work and how you can influence them.

- Volunteer to do any work you might find interesting. Do not be shy to ask what sorts of jobs there are, or suggest what you feel needs to be done.

In Canada, you could:

- Volunteer for your member of the legislative assembly (MLA) in most of Canada; your member of provincial parliament (MPP) in Ontario; your member of the national assembly (MNA) in Québec; your member in the house of assembly (MHA) in Newfoundland and Labrador; or your member of Parliament (MP).

In the United States, you could:

- Volunteer for your state representative or member of Congress.

Lobby governments

Lobbying means applying pressure on governments to influence them to take a stand on an issue. It can involve writing letters, attending meetings, and writing petitions. You can do this at the municipal, provincial, or federal levels.What other ways can you think of to influence governments? What issues do you think need addressing? Here are a few examples:

- Ask for funding to be allocated for the building of a playground in the community.
- Ask for tough penalties for companies that harm the environment by dumping hazardous wastes or toxic chemicals into rivers.
- Ask governments to take a stand on child labor. You might ask your federal government to trade only with countries that have compulsory education for all children.

TAKE ACTION! A Guide To Active Citizenship

Home	PART I	PART II
Preface, Contents	How To Get Involved: The Step-By-Step Process	The 'How To' Guide

HUMAN RIGHTS

On December 10, 1948, the General Assembly of the United Nations adopted and proclaimed the Universal Declaration of Human Rights. This document established that all people in the world have certain basic human rights, such as the right to food, simple housing, and political freedom, and that these rights should be protected and respected. The member states of the United Nations (nearly all the countries in the world) promised to uphold and enforce this important document.

Over half a century has passed since the Universal Declaration of Human Rights was

TAKe ACtiON! A Guide To Active Citizenship

Home	PART I	PART II
Preface, Contents	How To Get Involved: The Step-By-Step Process	The 'How To' Guide

introduced. What progress has been made during this time? Some people argue that very little has changed. Human rights abuses continue every day around the world. Here are just a few examples that outline ongoing or recent neglect of human rights:

- Nearly a billion people entered the 21st century unable to read a book or sign their names.
- According to the United Nations, close to one billion of the world's people are living in slum communities, representing 30 per cent of the world's urban population.
- Based on studies performed by the World Bank, women around the globe perform two-thirds of the world's work, receive less than one-tenth of the world's income, and own less than one one-hundredth of the world's property.

Clearly the issue of human rights is still an area that needs great attention. In order to uphold the Universal Declaration of Human Rights, everyone must help. One way that you can help is by organizing a Human Rights Awareness Day at your school. Education is the most important step in making this world a place where everyone's rights are respected.

Here are some other possibilities for action:

- Write letters to governments demanding that they protect human rights and link trade and economic development to human rights issues.
- Find out which major companies are human rights abusers. Research non-governmental organizations such as Verité and Human Rights Watch to find out which corporations have been linked to unfair labor practices. You may be surprised to find out which companies use sweatshop or child labor. Research a specific human rights abuser (a country or a company) and give a presentation to your class, student council, or local government. Education is the best way to stop human rights abuses.

What is the United Nations and what is its role?

The United Nations is an international organization made up of member countries that come together to discuss important world affairs. Over 190 countries, including Canada and the United States, belong to the United Nations. This body has helped to negotiate some very important international agreements, such as the United Nations Convention on Human Rights and the United Nations Convention on the Rights of the Child. Go to their website to get more information human rights and the United Nations itself.

TAKE ACTION! A Guide To Active Citizenship

Home	PART I	PART II
Preface, Contents	How To Get Involved: The Step-By-Step Process	The 'How To' Guide

How to Organize a Human Rights Awareness Day

Choose your issue

Become enthusiastic about organizing a Human Rights Awareness Day in your school.

Do some research

Research human rights violations around the world. In particular, see if there are any human rights abusers in your area, as there are even sweatshops in Canada and the United States. Make sure that your information is reliable and up-to-date (see the "Do Your Research" section beginning on page 5 in Part 1 for some helpful tips). You may want to contact an organization for help. Part 5 lists contact information for these organizations.

Get support from a teacher and your principal

Talk with your teacher or principal about the fact that you want to organize a Human Rights Awareness Day in your school. Tell them about the information you discovered during your research and explain why you feel it is important that your classmates learn about human rights.

Build a team

Speak to your friends at school and in your community about your Human Rights Awareness Day. Ask them to become involved. You may also want to ask some adults to help.

PART IV > Tackling Social Issues > Human Rights

| **PART III**
Where You Can Get Involved-
Everywhere! | **PART IV**
Tackling Social Issues | **PART V**
Sources And Resources,
End Notes |

Call a meeting

Hold a meeting once you have a team in order to make a plan of action.

Make a plan of action

Here are a few considerations you will want to keep in mind:
- What issues would you like to address during the Human Rights Awareness Day?
- How do you want your event to be set up? Plan a schedule for the day.
- Would you like to invite guest speakers to your event? Which groups could you contact?
- When will the event be held? The date you choose should not conflict with any other events being held at the school.
- How will the Human Rights Awareness Day be publicized?
- Will local media be invited to cover the event? (See the section "How to Work with the Media" beginning on page 82 in Part 3 for some helpful strategies.)

Take action and then review

Make your Human Rights Awareness Day a reality. Enjoy the day and have fun while learning more about important social issues. When the day is over, encourage everyone to continue learning about human rights issues.

Soon after the event, bring your team together to discuss what went well and what lessons were learned that the group can use to improve the next event. Thank everyone for participating.

Have fun!

Have fun while organizing the event, and enjoy spending time with your friends while participating in a worthwhile cause. Suggest a team activity to celebrate the successful organization of your Human Rights Awareness Day.

PART IV > **Tackling Social Issues** > **Human Rights**

| **PART III** Where You Can Get Involved-Everywhere! | **PART IV** Tackling Social Issues | **PART V** Sources And Resources, End Notes |

Profile: Sheena Kamal

Simple ideas which inspire the mind have a way of spreading. It was such an idea, read in a newspaper, that made Sheena Kamal from Toronto, Canada, realize that her life would be about helping others. One day, when she was only 15 years old, Sheena read about Free The Children and was inspired by the simple message that youth have the ability to be leaders of today, not just tomorrow.

Something in her mind clicked, and from that point forward Sheena became a dedicated volunteer. Soon after, Sheena embarked on a trip to Jamaica, where she worked with children living in poverty. Deeply touched by the hard lives the children faced, Sheena felt her own life changing. When she returned to Canada, she began speaking to her friends and peers at R.H. King Academy about what she'd seen, and organized them to become socially involved. Shortly thereafter, Sheena became director of Free The Children's Toronto Youth in Action Group.

As she became more informed about poverty, she saw that it was everywhere in the world, in Canada as well as Jamaica. The fact that there were children and youth living on her city's streets was the most devastating revelation of all. It seemed so unfair, because children have no control over poverty, and Sheena wanted to raise awareness of their collective plight.

It was a large task, but she was ready for the challenge. Her first step was to coordinate a project to support street youth by providing them with basic living kits, things to keep them healthy and comfortable through Canada's changing and often harsh seasons. She invited two speakers, each of whom had at one time been homeless, to help her group compile a list of useful items to include in the basic living kits. To distribute the supplies, which included clothing, bottled water, and soap, to people living on the streets of Toronto, Sheena contacted a local charity for the homeless that conducted street runs to aid the homeless.

Sheena then arranged for a group of young people to go on the street runs too. It was an education on homelessness that you couldn't get from reading a book. Not only were they able to see what life on the streets was like, but the youth also had the chance to interact with the homeless and sometimes even to develop friendships.

For her work as a youth activist and community leader, Sheena was awarded a TD Canada Trust Scholarship for outstanding community leadership.

CHILDREN'S RIGHTS

It is important for young people to understand their rights. In 1989, world leaders gathered together to determine the rights of children. The result was the United Nations Convention on the Rights of the Child. This is an international agreement that establishes the rights of children and young people who are under the age of 18. Over 190 countries around the world have accepted and have promised to enforce this important agreement. No other international human rights treaty has been more widely adopted on an international level.

The convention can be divided into four categories of rights:

1. **Playing a Part:** This section of the agreement says young people must be included in the decision-making process on important issues that affect them. The document also says that young people have the freedom to join with other young people to protect their rights and to express their opinions.

2. **Reaching Their Potential:** This section of the agreement protects important social rights of youth. Included in this list are the right to have access to education and the right to protect their culture and identity.

3. **Living Well: The Right to Survival:** This section of the agreement says that there are certain basic things that all young people must have, such as adequate food and shelter, a reasonable standard of living, and access to health care.

4. **Being Free from Harm:** This section of the agreement says that all young people should be protected from abuse, neglect, economic exploitation (child labor), torture, abduction (kidnapping and trafficking), and prostitution. So far, however, the rights that were agreed upon in this important convention have yet to be upheld in some places. Right now, as you read this, millions of children around the world are being exploited and abused, while some governments continue to break their promises to take "all appropriate measures" to defend the rights of these young people. All children deserve the right to be a kid and have their rights protected. The United Nations Convention on the Rights of the Child was a big step, but it was not enough. The good news is that you can help. One way you can help children is by raising funds to build a school in the developing world. Primary schooling is guaranteed under the United Nations Convention on the Rights of the Child, yet millions of children around the world do not have the opportunity to go to school because there is simply no school available in their communities. Education is the key to breaking the cycle of poverty and ending the exploitation of children. You will find out how to raise money to build a school on the next page.

Some other possibilities for action:

- Join an organization concerned with children's rights. See Part 5 for contact information.
- You can write to the government in the United States urging them to support the ratification of the United Nations Convention on the Rights of the Child. The United States, which has signed but not ratified the Convention, is one of only two countries in the world that has not adopted this treaty. The other country is Somalia, which currently has no recognized government.
- You can write letters and organize petitions to send to government officials to pressure them to make children's rights a priority.

How to Raise Funds to Build a School

Choose an issue

Become enthusiastic about building a primary school in the developing world for children who otherwise would not be given the opportunity to have an education.

Do some research

Research topics such as education, child labor, and child poverty (refer to the "Do Your Research" section beginning on page 5 in Part 1 for some helpful tips). You may also want to contact Free The Children for help (see Part 5 for contact information).

Build a team

Involve your friends or give a presentation in front of your class about how education can put an end to the exploitation of children. Ask for their help. A group of people can raise funds much more easily than you can by yourself.

PART III
Where You Can Get Involved-
Everywhere!

PART IV
Tackling Social Issues

PART V
Sources And Resources,
End Notes

Call a meeting

Speak to your friends at school and in your community about participating in building a school in a developing country. Ask them to become involved and meet with you to make a plan of action. You may also want to ask some adults for help.

Make a plan of action
Here are a few considerations you will want to keep in mind:

- The cost of building a one-room school in a developing country varies from region to region. The cost, however, begins at $5,000 (in United States dollars) and $6,000 (in Canadian dollars), respectively. Contact Free The Children to get an exact amount depending on where, geographically, you would like the school to be built. This is a large amount of money; but it is not an impossible target. In fact, Free The Children has already built over 500 schools with the help of enterprising people like you. Think about how you will fundraise to build this school.
- With whom do you need to work to make your fundraiser successful? Which adults can you contact who can help raise your group to raise funds?
- What materials will you need for your fundraiser? How many young people do you want to become involved in this campaign?
- Refer to the section "101 Fundraisers" beginning on page 108 in Part 2 for fundraising suggestions.
- How will you advertise your fundraiser? Will you invite the media to your event?

Take action and then review

Make your fundraiser(s) a reality. Tell people about the event and why it is such a worthy cause. Make sure that people find out about your project and that they know how to contact you.

When your event is complete, and you've sent your funds to Free The Children, you will have taken the exciting first step toward building a school. When construction is finished, Free The Children will send you and your group pictures of and information about the school that you helped to build. Share this information with all of the people who were involved in the fundraiser. Your supporters will then see the effect of their contributions and will be more likely to help in the future.

TAKE ACTION! A Guide To Active Citizenship

Home	PART I	PART II
Preface, Contents	How To Get Involved: The Step-By-Step Process	The 'How To' Guide

Soon after your event, bring your team together and discuss what aspects of the fundraiser were successful, as well as lessons the group learned that can be used to improve the next event. Remember to thank everyone who participated in your event.

Have fun!

Have fun while organizing the event, and enjoy spending time with your friends while participating in a worthwhile cause. Suggest a team activity to celebrate the hard work and dedication it took to contribute to the education of children in the developing world.

Profile: Sally Hakim

In the past, Sally Hakim's school had a reputation for gangs and violence. Today, however, it is a model that others emulate.

A student at Monarch Park Collegiate Institute, from Toronto, Canada, Sally was always passionate about education. She loved learning, and after being elected student president in Grade 11, Sally made a discovery that changed her life, as well as the future of her school.

At a student council meeting one day, Sally learned of a local organization that focused on education as the key to breaking the cycle of poverty. Interested in what they had to offer, she invited a speaker from the organization to a school assembly. After an inspiring speech that focused on the lack of education in developing countries, staff and students alike were inspired. They joined forces to form a committee, setting the lofty goal of building a school in Kenya.

Immediately, Sally and her classmates had to overcome the challenge of fundraising in a low-income school. They also had to prove to others that the goal was possible. Pushing all doubts aside, their committee of nearly 50 youth leaders started weekly coin collections, held food sales, and worked with clubs and classes. From the athletic department who ran their own fundraisers, to the special education class that counted the coin drive money, everyone got involved.

At the end of the year, Sally and Monarch Park Collegiate Institute had done what many thought impossible, they had raised enough to build a school in Kenya. Many would be happy with this outcome, but for Monarch Park this was only the beginning.

Since then, the school's students have helped build a second school in Kenya, as well as raised $5,000 for medical supplies for Sri Lankan tsunami victims. A reward of their efforts and a sign of their commitment, in 2006 Sally and 20 of her classmates traveled to Kenya to build (with their own hands!) the second school for which they had fundraised.

Coming together to raise awareness about the importance of education has transformed the culture at Monarch Park. Hand-in-hand with the increase in civic engagement, the school has seen a remarkable decrease in violence and bullying. Sally attributed this to a shift in how students see themselves. "Students have begun to realize that the ability to make positive change is within each of us, regardless of where we come from, what we did in the past, where we live, or our race or nationality."

In her final year at Monarch Park, Sally was school president once again, determined as ever to support education projects and to cultivate the growing pride of Monarch Park students in their school community.

THE ENVIRONMENT

Earth is our home, and it is very important to protect it.

If we pollute the air and the water, we will harm the plants and animals of the world as well as ourselves. Everyone can make a contribution to preserving our environment by thinking about how our actions—such as how we grow our food—affect the planet, and how adjusting our behavior might help to remedy the situation.

If there is an environmental issue that interests you, do some research to find out more. Consider these issues:
* air pollution and human health
* animal rights and wildlife protection
* biodiversity
* deforestation and clear-cutting
* garbage and waste reduction
* global warming and climate change
* national parks and land conservation
* organic agriculture and soil erosion
* over-fishing
* pesticide and herbicide use
* water quality and conservation

These are all important and complicated issues. Our planet is in trouble and unless we take action, the damage will be irreversible. The good news is that you can help.

One way you can help is by planting an organic garden at your school (see the next page for more information.) Here are some other possibilities for action:
* Invite guest speakers to talk to your school about environmental issues.
* Organize a tree-planting day.
* Organize a garbage-free lunch day at your school.
* Start a compost pile. If you do it right, it won't smell!
* Promote waste reduction and a recycling program at your school.
* Organize a clean up the park day (make sure that you get permission from an adult and that there is adult supervision).

TAKE ACTiON! A Guide To Active Citizenship

| **Home** Preface, Contents | **PART I** How To Get Involved: The Step-By-Step Process | **PART II** The 'How To' Guide |

How to Organize a School Organic Garden

Choose an issue

Become enthusiastic about helping to protect the environment. Choose which area of the environment you would like to focus on, such as reducing water pollution, human health hazards, and soil erosion, by producing healthy organic foods in an organic garden.

Do some research

Find out why organic agriculture is important and how choosing to grow and eat local organic foods can help the environment. Also, try to estimate how far the food on your dinner plate has to travel before it reaches your family's grocery store. The farther the distance, the more pollution is created. That is why producing food locally is so important.

Think of what you will need to plant your own school garden. For example:

* a sunny patch of ground or a safe roof-top location in which to plant raised beds.
* a generous supply of organic compost and well-rotted manure.
* tools (human powered) and someone to show you how to use them safely.
* a source of clean water to keep your plants from getting thirsty.
* someone who knows about organic gardening to mentor your group.
* a simple storage facility, like someone's refrigerator or root cellar, in which to store your harvest.

Get support from a teacher and your principal

Talk to a teacher and your principal about the research you have done and about the importance of having an organic garden in your school. You may wish to involve an adult mentor who has knowledge of organic gardening.

PART IV > Tackling Social Issues > Children's Rights

PART III
Where You Can Get Involved-
Everywhere!

PART IV
Tackling Social Issues

PART V
Sources And Resources,
End Notes

Build a team

Involve your friends or give a presentation in front of your class about the environment and about organic gardening. Ask for their help. There is strength in numbers.

Call a meeting

Speak to your friends at school and in your community about helping to plan your organic garden. Ask them to become involved and meet with you to make a plan of action. You will also want to ask some knowledgeable adults for help.

Make a plan of action

Address the following issues when you are organizing your organic garden:

- Should a letter be sent home to students' families explaining about your plans for a school garden?
- If you have a cafeteria/dining hall in your school, is there some way you could involve it in your plans?
- What kind of garden do you want to grow? You could grow flowers, root vegetables, salad greens, herbs, heritage vegetables, or berries.
- How will you involve other students in your garden so that they feel responsible and proud of it? How much do you need to involve your student government in the process?
- How are you going to keep this project sustainable (keep it going year after year)?
- How are you going to use your garden to teach others about environmental issues like water pollution, soil erosion, biodiversity, pesticide and herbicide use, or waste reduction?

Take action and then review

Make your organic garden a reality. Enjoy knowing that you have done something valuable to help the environment.

Draw a poster of your garden and post it in a high-traffic area of the school. Let people know where it is located and when different foods are harvested from the garden. Announce the benefits of local and organic gardening over your school's PA system. You will be amazed at the response! When people understand that they can help the environment by simply changing their routines, they will be encouraged to make organic foods a habit.

TAKE ACTION! A Guide To Active Citizenship

Home	PART I	PART II
Preface, Contents	How To Get Involved: The Step-By-Step Process	The 'How To' Guide

Soon after the event, review with the team what went well and what was learned in order to make next year's garden an even greater success. Remember to thank everyone who helped you with the garden.

Have fun!

Enjoy knowing that your efforts have resulted in more healthy organic food being produced locally. You have made a difference, so consider celebrating your contribution by organizing a team activity, such as cooking a tasty group dinner using foods that were grown locally and organically.

PART IV > Tackling Social Issues > Children's Rights

| **PART III**
Where You Can Get Involved-
Everywhere! | **PART IV**
Tackling Social Issues | **PART V**
Sources And Resources,
End Notes |

Profile: Jean-Dominic Lévesque-René

Jean-Dominic Lévesque-René's battle for a cleaner and safer environment began unexpectedly. In 1994, he was watching television when he felt a bump on the side of his neck. His parents took him to the hospital for tests, and soon discovered that he had non-Hodgkins lymphoma, a form of cancer. Only 10 years old at the time, Jean-Dominic was told that he had a 50 per cent chance of survival and would be in chemotherapy treatment for 49 weeks. Being hooked up to a machine was lonely and strange, but it gave Jean-Dominic time to think. He began to wonder, "How did I get this cancer?"

More than half of the area of Ile-Bizard, the suburb in Montreal, Canada, where Jean-Dominic grew up, is covered with golf courses, which use a lot of pesticides to keep the fairways free of weeds. After stumbling across a pamphlet linking cancer to pesticide exposure, Jean-Dominic remembered having unexplained nosebleeds and rashes as a child, and noticed that a number of his friends in the cancer ward also came from Ile-Bizard. Jean-Dominic decided that others should know about this frightening connection. He organized a youth demonstration calling for a ban on pesticides and repeatedly brought his request to town hall meetings. He made the news, but when the mayor did not take him seriously, Jean-Dominic did not give up. He could not ignore the evidence he saw around him. He set to work to prove what he believed, that the pesticides being used in his community had caused his cancer.

In 1998, he pushed the researchers at his hospital to conduct a study, and their statistics showed that the cancer rate among children in Ile-Bizard was ten times the national rate. Jean-Dominic began organizing letter writing and petition campaigns, and went on to speak to various associations, student groups, and government officials. He widened the scope of his crusade, asking for a pesticide ban not just in Ile-Bizard, but throughout the country as well. Jean-Dominic found it difficult to be patient when change seemed to come so slowly. His persistence paid off, though, when after six years, the town council of Ile-Bizard finally banned pesticides. In 2003, the Minister of the Environment of Quebec presented the new provincial pesticide management code. The code, which is also the strongest law in the world concerning health and the environment, bans the non-essential use of pesticides on Quebec lawns and public green spaces, including schools and daycare centers. In addition, the government of Quebec has decided to use a non-toxic bacteria alternative to chemical insecticide in preventing the West Nile Virus.

Jean-Dominic's dedication has been recognized with multiple awards, including the YTV Terry Fox Award for Environmental Activism and the Canadian Order for Youth. In 2001, he was elected to the Global 500 Youth Environmental Roll of Honour of the United Nations Environment Programme. His crusade was a battle not only for his own life, but also for the health and lives of others, especially children.

HUNGER

Hunger is one of the most important social issues facing the world today. Deaths from hunger and related diseases total 10 million each year—exceeding the amount from AIDS, malaria and tuberculosis combined.

This is despite the fact that there is more than enough food currently produced on the planet to feed our current population. Clearly, this is not a matter of lack of resources. Food is always available to those who can afford to buy it.

There is no one reason why world hunger exists. Contributing factors include politics, distribution, economics, environmental degradation, and production. Even though Canada and the United States are among the world's richest countries, hunger is still a major North American problem. In Canada, an estimated 3.7 million people are food insecure. (Food insecurity means a lack of access to enough food to meet basic needs due to poverty.) In the United States, 38 million people suffer the same fate. Globally, there are an estimated 850 million hungry people in the world.

You can help reduce these numbers. One way that you can help is by organizing a Halloween for Hunger campaign. Instead of trick-or-treating for candy this coming October 31, collect food for your local food bank.

Here are some other possibilities for action:
- Do not waste food. Make sure to take only as much food as you are going to eat. This is something that everyone can work on.
- Organize a can drive through your school or place of worship.
- Organize a day of fasting (not eating) to raise awareness about hunger. Make sure that you have an adult advisor helping you, and that your parents or guardians are aware of what you are doing.

How to Organize a Halloween for Hunger Campaign

A Halloween for Hunger campaign involves collecting non-perishable food supplies at Halloween instead of candy. The canned goods can then be donated to local food banks to help people who are hungry.

PART III
Where You Can Get Involved-
Everywhere!

PART IV
Tackling Social Issues

PART V
Sources And Resources,
End Notes

Choose an issue

Become enthusiastic about helping the poor around the world who are hungry by organizing a Halloween for Hunger event.

Do some research

Find out about hunger in Canada, the United States, and around the world. Visit websites such as that of the United Nations World Food Programme (WFP) or the Food and Agriculture Organization of the United Nations (FAO) for useful facts and statistics. Contact your local food bank to find out about hunger in your area.

Build a team

Involve your friends or give a presentation in front of your class about Halloween for Hunger. Ask if your fellow classmates want to become involved. If more people are part of your team, you will be able to collect more canned food for hungry people.

Call a meeting

Hold a meeting once you have a team in order to make a plan of action.

Make a plan of action

Here are some aspects of the campaign that you will want to keep in mind when developing your plan of action:

- Where will the food go once it is collected?
- People will need to be informed ahead of time that you will be collecting food instead of candy on Halloween. Put up flyers and posters around the community, informing people when you will be collecting and that you are looking for healthy canned or non-perishable foods. One good idea is to put up a poster in or near grocery stores (ask for permission first).
- How will you carry all of the canned goods once they are collected? Will everyone meet in a central location to make sorting of the cans easier?
- Do you want to tell the local media about your campaign? Do you want to spread the campaign to other schools and other communities?

TAKE ACTION! A Guide To Active Citizenship

Home	PART I	PART II
Preface, Contents	How To Get Involved: The Step-By-Step Process	The 'How To' Guide

- You may want to figure out which neighborhood each volunteer will cover. After all, you do not want to be asking the same people twice and you do not want to miss anyone. Try mapping out the community and assign different streets or areas to individual volunteers.

- Remember, if you are going to houses of people you do not know, have an adult accompany you.

Take action and then review

Make your Halloween for Hunger campaign a success. Collect the non-perishable food items while having fun dressing up in Halloween costumes—you could even dress-up as vegetables! Feel good in knowing that you are making a difference in the lives of others. Once the event is over, consider displaying posters to inform people in your community how much food was collected and to thank them for their contributions.

Soon after the event, review with your team what worked well and what could be improved the next time you conduct a similar campaign. What steps might be taken to sustain the campaign year-round.

Have fun!

A Halloween for Hunger event is intended to be fun. To bolster enthusiasm, consider hosting a Halloween party before your volunteers go collecting food in the community.

Halloween for Hunger

Halloween for Hunger started with just a small group of people who wanted to make a difference. Since then, the idea has spread so that now Halloween for Hunger collects millions of cans of food all over the world, even in countries that do not celebrate Halloween! Contact the local media about the food that you raised so that the idea can continue to spread. To learn more about Halloween for Hunger, visit www.freethechildren.com.

TAKE ACTION! A Guide To Active Citizenship

| **Home** Preface, Contents | **PART I** How To Get Involved: The Step-By-Step Process | **PART II** The 'How To' Guide |

PART IV > Tackling Social Issues > Hunger

| **PART III** Where You Can Get Involved- Everywhere! | **PART IV** Tackling Social Issues | **PART V** Sources And Resources, End Notes |

Profile: Anina Tweed

In Grade 10, Anina Tweed watched *It Takes a Child*, a movie which documents Craig Kielburger's childhood trip to Southeast Asia where he met with and learned from child laborers. What Anina saw inspired her and a question formed in her head. "If a 12-year-old boy can start Free The Children, then why can't I, at 15, start a club at my school?"

Though Anina was happy that the student body at Nevada Union High School in Grass Valley, USA, was socially active, she wanted to do something with an international focus.

Though it had humble beginnings, like Free The Children, Anina was determined that her group would "do something big and see a positive outcome."

Her first step was to recruit her good friend, Alicia, and together they formed the Nevada Union Youth in Action Group. Then, as a group of two, they recruited more members, and more, in spite of the skepticism they sometimes faced from others. Undeterred, Anina and Alicia told every person they saw about their club and before long they succeeded in recruiting 24 eager and dedicated members.

As their first action, the club embraced a seasonal campaign to combat local and global hunger: Halloween for Hunger. Decked out in costumes, Nevada Union students took to the streets on Halloween night, trick-or-treating for canned goods instead of candy. (A little candy may have been handed out as well…) With an ambitious goal of 1,000 cans, the night began. Trip after trip, up and down neighborhood streets, their treat bags filled with donated food. Before they knew it, Anina's brother's van was full to bursting with food bank offerings, far exceeding their goal and leading to a successful night for both the group and the community food bank.

Not a group to rest on its achievements, Anina and the Nevada Union Youth in Action Group have already begun their newest project: helping to build a school in war-ravaged Sierra Leone. For Anina, this is a natural next step for her and her group, continuing her social action against hunger and poverty by providing children in Sierra Leone with a much-needed education.

Halloween for Hunger and now schoolbuilding, Anina and Nevada Union are proof that though change can happen slowly, it doesn't need to.

POVERTY

Poverty is one of the largest and most complex problems currently facing the world. The reason why poverty is such a key area of concern is because it either causes or contributes to nearly all other social issues discussed in this book. For example, one of the main reasons why children die of hunger or why they cannot go to school and receive an education is because they are poor.

Here are some statistics about poverty around the world:

- According to the United Nations, 28 per cent of the people living in the world's developing and transitional countries live in absolute poverty with incomes of less than $1 per day.
- According to UNICEF's *2006 State of the World's Children* report, to provide every child in the world with quality primary education would cost between $7 and $17 billion per year—a small amount compared to other government expenditures such as global military spending.
- One out of every six, or approximately 1.2 million, Canadian children lives below the poverty line.
- More than 11 million American children live in poor families.

Education is the key to breaking the cycle of poverty

An education gives children the opportunity to have a better future. With the skills obtained through an education, children will be able to receive higher paying jobs (when they are older) and be better able to support their present and future families. Parents also need help, and Free The Children's Adopt a Village campaign attempts to assist them by supporting their efforts to improve their job opportunities and family income. Find out how to adopt a village on the next page.

Here are some other ways you can act to combat poverty:

- Volunteer at your local food bank or homeless shelter.
- Encourage government officials through letter-writing campaigns to support legislation that will eliminate the debts of developing countries.
- Volunteer overseas and help to build a school, dig a well, or teach English in a local primary school.

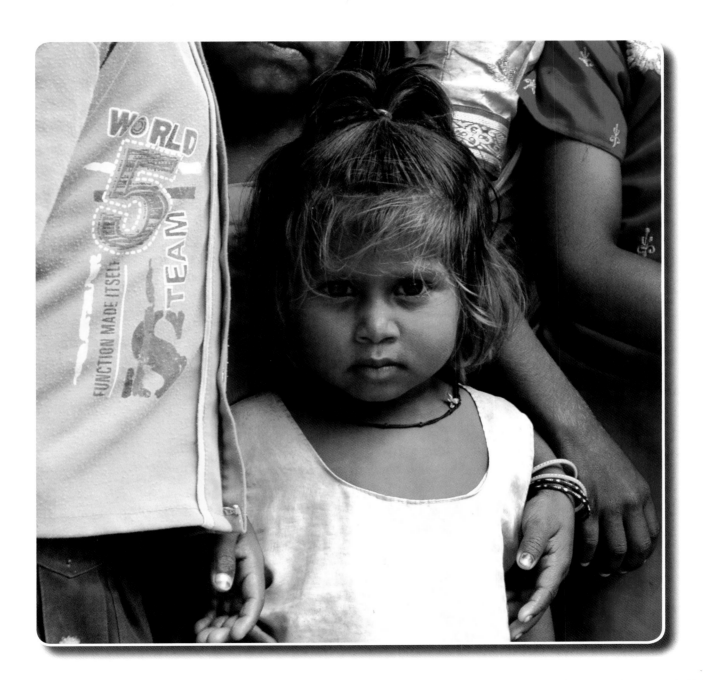

TAKE ACTION! A Guide To Active Citizenship

| **Home**
Preface, Contents | **PART I**
How To Get Involved:
The Step-By-Step Process | **PART II**
The 'How To' Guide |

How to Adopt a Village

Choose an issue

Become enthusiastic about helping to create a more just and equitable world. Commit yourself to taking action by raising funds to support children and families in developing countries.

Do some research

Research topics associated with development, such as child labor, child poverty, clean water, and food security. See Part 5 for some organizations you may want to research.

Build a team

Involve your friends or give a presentation in front of your class about Adopt a Village. Explain that there are many children who cannot go to school simply because their parents and relatives cannot afford to send them. Ask if your classmates want to become involved. If more people are part of your team, you will be able to help more children attend school.

Call a meeting

Hold a meeting once you have a team in order to make a plan of action on how you will organize your campaign.

Make a plan of action

Here are some questions to keep in mind when organizing your campaign:

- How will you help families send their children to school? With Adopt a Village you have many options. You can help parents earn better incomes. You can help to build community wells. You can build or equip a school, or provide teacher training. Or you can provide children and their families with access to quality health care.
- How will you raise funds for your chosen area of interest?
- Will you need brochures or promotional materials to explain Adopt a Village to others?
- How will you reach your fundraising goals?
- How will you keep your team, school, or community motivated?

PART IV > Tackling Social Issues > Poverty

| **PART III**
Where You Can Get Involved-
Everywhere! | **PART IV**
Tackling Social Issues | **PART V**
Sources And Resources,
End Notes |

Take action and review

To make your Adopt a Village campaign a success, your group will need to think of creative fundraising ideas that will capture the hearts of your community members. (Refer to the section "101 Fundraisers" beginning on page 108 in Part 3 for fundraising suggestions.) Whatever component of Adopt a Village you choose to fundraise for, remember that each step is important to helping children attend school. Once your goals have been reached, and you've celebrated your success, assemble your team to discuss any lessons the group learned that will make future campaigns even more successful. Be sure to discuss what went well and to thank everyone who helped your team reach its goals.

Have fun!

Congratulate yourselves on making a difference in the lives of children by holding a fun dinner to celebrate your team's Adopt a Village success story.

Adopt a Village

Adopt a Village tackles local poverty by helping children and their families to meet their basic human needs. Adopt a Village began in 2004 with the goal of helping Sri Lankan tsunami victims to rebuild after the devastating natural disaster. Today, however, Adopt a Village aids in the development of children, families, and their communities across Africa and Asia. To learn more about Adopt a Village, visit www.freethechildren.com.

TAKE ACTION! A Guide To Active Citizenship

| **Home** Preface, Contents | **PART I** How To Get Involved: The Step-By-Step Process | **PART II** The 'How To' Guide |

Profile: Rachel Herold

Because of her sister's early social involvement, Rachel Herold, a Grade 12 student at Scarsdale High School in New York City, USA, was keenly aware about the tragic challenges poverty imposes on children. Her sister's actions made her wonder about how she, too, might help lift young people out of poverty.

"We have the power and responsibility to do something," Rachel asserted with confidence. "We can make a difference!" Rachel took this belief to heart, leading the Scarsdale High School Youth in Action Group first as education coordinator and then as president.

She had big shoes to fill, because when Rachel stepped into the role of leader, the Scarsdale group had already built a school in Kenya. Yet she was determined not to let that stand in the way of achieving more. Armed with the knowledge that the poverty many Kenyan children face prevents them from attending school, Rachel decided that she and the Scarsdale group would help the same village where they had previously built a primary school. If poverty was the challenge, then the Scarsdale group would provide the village's families with ways to eliminate poverty through the Adopt a Village campaign.

Already established as a fundraising dynamo, the group held two carnivals for local youth, featuring creative activities such as musical Twister, tennis ball bowling, an animal bean bag toss, and pin the tail on the goat! On top of this, a dinner dance, a silent auction, and the Vow of Silence campaign helped the group surpass its goal of US $5000!

Because of their tenacity, Rachel and Scarsdale High School helped to empower women in Kenya with the ability to bring themselves out of poverty through alternative income projects. Now, mothers given milking animals and sewing machines are better able to support their families. With parents earning more income, children can learn to read in school instead of working. It is a simple formula.

After graduation, Rachel passed on the reins of the Scarsdale High School Youth in Action Group to up-and-coming young leaders. As it was with her sister, now Rachel and her peer's examples will drive the actions of another generation to continue doing good deeds with gentle kindness.

HIV/AIDS

HIV (human immunodeficiency virus) is a virus that destroys the body's capacity for immunity and results in AIDS (acquired immune deficiency syndrome). AIDS is a disease that is causing great concern around the world, in both developed and developing countries. There are over 38 million people infected with HIV worldwide. Although progress has been made in caring for HIV/AIDS patients, there is no known cure. The AIDS virus is spreading particularly rapidly in developing countries. The main reason for the higher rates of infection in developing countries is a lack of education. One of the main reasons why people get infected is simply because they do not realize that they are at risk.

How do people get infected?

Having unprotected sexual contact or sharing needles with an infected person causes the majority of the infections of HIV. Also, mothers who have the disease can pass the illness on to their children before birth, during birth, or while breastfeeding. Blood transfusions can also cause infection, although this is extremely rare now due to blood screening. These are the only scientifically proven ways of contracting HIV.

Here are a few United Nations statistics and facts about HIV/AIDS around the world:

- There were an estimated 4.1 million new HIV infections in the year 2005 alone.
- In 2005 an estimated 2.8 million people lost their lives to AIDS.
- Africa remains the global epicentre of the AIDS pandemic. South Africa's AIDS epidemic—where an estimated 5.5 million people were living with HIV in 2005 - shows no evidence of a decline.
- Every minute of every day, a child under the age of 15 becomes infected with HIV. Meanwhile, 90 percent of the more than 5 million children who have been infected were born in Africa.
- Although women comprise about half of all people living with HIV worldwide, girls and women are made particularly vulnerable to HIV by conditions of gender inequality.

PART III
Where You Can Get Involved-
Everywhere!

PART IV
Tackling Social Issues

PART V
Sources And Resources,
End Notes

TAKE Action! A Guide To Active Citizenship

| **Home** Preface, Contents | **PART I** How To Get Involved: The Step-By-Step Process | **PART II** The 'How To' Guide |

In May and June of 2006, a strong declaration on HIV/AIDS was approved by over 140 members of the United Nations General Assembly. This declaration recognizes that HIV/AIDS is "a global crisis" and calls for "a global response." This means that we all must work together to solve this problem. There are many things that you can do to help. One way is to organize an HIV/AIDS Awareness Day.

Here are some other possibilities for action:

- Volunteer at a local hospital or AIDS hospice and help care for AIDS patients.
- Raise money to give to organizations such as the Stephen Lewis Foundation and the National AIDS Fund. These organizations provide relief to AIDS patients and are involved in HIV/AIDS prevention.
- Write letters to major pharmaceutical companies (drug companies) telling them that you think they should provide AIDS medication to the developing world free of charge.

How to Organize an HIV/AIDS Awareness Day

Choose an issue

Decide that you are passionate about joining the global campaign to rid the world of HIV/AIDS and that you want to educate people about the disease through an AIDS awareness day.

Do some research

Obtain information about HIV/AIDS as it relates to your country and to the world. Conduct an Internet search to locate the websites for the Joint UN Programme on HIV/AIDS (UNAIDS), among other sites. Make sure that your information is accurate and current.

Get support from a teacher and your principal

Talk to your teacher or principal about what you would like to do. Share what you discovered through your research and explain why you feel it is important that your classmates learn about this important social issue. You may also want to find a teacher to work with you.

PART IV > Tackling Social Issues > HIV / AIDS

| **PART III** Where You Can Get Involved- Everywhere! | **PART IV** Tackling Social Issues | **PART V** Sources And Resources, End Notes |

Build a team

Make a presentation to your class about the HIV/AIDS Awareness Day. Share your research information and ask for volunteers to become involved in this event.

Call a meeting

Hold a meeting once you have a team in order to make a plan of action.

Make a Plan of Action

Consider the following when you are developing your plan of action:
* Think about how you want your event to be set up. Plan a schedule for the day.
* Would you like to invite guest speakers to your event? Which groups could you contact?
* Choose a date for the event that will not conflict with any other events that are being held at the school.
* Determine ways to publicize the HIV/AIDS Awareness Day.

Take Action and then review

Have a successful and educational HIV/AIDS Awareness Day. When the day is over, encourage everyone to continue learning more about the issue of HIV/AIDS.

Soon after the event, review the strengths and weaknesses of the HIV/AIDS Awareness Day in order to improve next year's event. Do not forget to thank everyone who was involved.

Have fun!

Have fun while organizing the event and enjoy spending time with your friends while participating in such a worthwhile cause. Suggest a fun activity that you and your team can do to celebrate a great HIV/AIDS Awareness Day.

PART III
Where You Can Get Involved-
Everywhere!

PART IV
Tackling Social Issues

PART V
Sources And Resources,
End Notes

Profile: Nkosi Johnson

In February 1989 a boy was born with HIV into a life of hardship in KwaZulu Natal, South Africa. His birth name was Xolani Nkosi, but the world would come to know him as Nkosi Johnson, "the courageous boy who moved a continent" for helping to break the silence about HIV and AIDS.

At 12 years old, he inspired millions of people around the world by being open about his disease in a country where families and communities often shun people with HIV/AIDS.

In 1997, Nkosi first gained the attention of South Africans when he and his foster mother, Gail Johnson, successfully challenged a primary school that refused to admit him because he had AIDS. Their fight led to a country-wide policy forbidding schools from discriminating against HIV-positive children and to guidelines for how schools should treat infected students.

From that point forward, Nkosi spoke out to raise awareness of HIV/AIDS and challenged people to re-examine their fears of people living with the disease. Nkosi attracted worldwide attention when he spoke at the 13th International AIDS conference in the South African city of Durban, asking for compassion for HIV/AIDS victims and urging the government to provide HIV-positive pregnant women with drugs to prevent the transmission of the virus to their infants. This was an issue that was close to his heart.

Nkosi's birth mother, Nonthlanthla Nkosi, had felt compelled to give him up to the loving care of Gail Johnson when she became too ill with AIDS to properly care for him. It was Nkosi's wish that HIV/AIDS should not come between other mothers and their children, so in 1999 Gail founded Nkosi's Havens, a community of homes for HIV-positive mothers and their children that continues to grow and expand its programs.

In 2001, Nkosi died of an AIDS-related disease. It was a tragedy felt by all who knew him or had been touched by his words. "It is a great pity that this young man has died; he was very bold," said former South African President Nelson Mandela, who has called Nkosi an "icon of the struggle for life."

Nkosi was a young ambassador who challenged people to treat those suffering from HIV/AIDS with dignity and respect. It earned him lasting recognition as a global ambassador for humanity. His words, spoken at the 13th International AIDS conference still ring true: "Do all you can with what you have in the time you have in the place you are."

Source: Adapted from: Susanna Loof, "Nkosi Johnson, 12, Dies; S. African AIDS Activist: Boy Born With HIV Urged Openness," The Washington Post. Saturday, June 2, 2001; pg. B07.

TAKe ACtiON!   A Guide To Active Citizenship

| **Home**
Preface, Contents | **PART I**
How To Get Involved:
The Step-By-Step Process | **PART II**
The 'How To' Guide |

PEACE

Our history books are filled with stories of war, and even though we tend to study wars and famous battles, we very rarely celebrate and study peace and cooperation. The world can achieve much more through working together than it can through conflict, yet war is often chosen to settle disputes when peaceful negotiations would be a better choice. One of the reasons why the issue of peace is so urgent is because we live in an age of nuclear weapons, genocide, child soldiers, terrorism, landmines, and growing military spending.

Here are some facts on global military spending:

- World military expenditure in 2005 is estimated to have reached $1 trillion. A small fraction of this money would be enough to solve nearly all of the world's problems, including hunger, illiteracy, and many environmental issues.
- The United States is responsible for nearly half of the world's total military spending.
- Of the more than 30,000 intact nuclear warheads belonging to the world's eight nuclear weapon states, the vast majority are in the United States or Russia.
- The United Nations estimates that more than 110 million active landmines are scattered in 68 countries. Our world does not have to be constantly at war. Peace is possible, but we must work together. There are many ways you can help. One way is by organizing a War is Not a Game campaign in your school or community. War is Not a Game encourages people to boycott war-related toys and video games. The purpose of this campaign is to help people realize that while some children play war, many children actually fight in wars as child soldiers. This campaign raises awareness not only about the exploitation of children, but also about the importance of peace.

Here are some other possibilities for action:

- Start a peace club in your school to educate others about the benefits of peace.
- Write to your government officials and encourage them to promote peace, to support
- nuclear disarmament, and to ban landmines.
- Hold a Peace Day at your school in which you celebrate peace heroes like Nelson Mandela, Lester B. Pearson, Mother Teresa, and Mahatma Gandhi.

TAKE ACTiON! A Guide To Active Citizenship

| **Home** Preface, Contents | **PART I** How To Get Involved: The Step-By-Step Process | **PART II** The 'How To' Guide |

How to Organize a War is Not a Game Campaign

Choose an issue

Become enthusiastic about creating a more peaceful world and commit yourself to organizing a War is Not a Game campaign in your school.

Do some research

Gain more knowledge on the issue and learn about child soldiers, global military spending, nuclear weapons, and landmines. Visit the website of the Nuclear Age Peace Foundation and that of the United Nations as a starting point. Make sure the information you obtain is both accurate and current.

Get support from a teacher and your principal

Talk to a teacher or your principal about the fact that you want to organize a War is Not a Game campaign in your school. Demonstrate what you discovered through your research and explain why you feel it is important that your classmates learn about this important social issue.

Build a team

Make a presentation to your class about war and the sub-issues of nuclear weapons, landmines, and children in armed conflict. Share your research information and request the help of volunteers.

Call a meeting

Hold a meeting once you have a team in order to develop a plan of action.

PART IV > Tackling Social Issues > Peace

PART III	PART IV	PART V
Where You Can Get Involved-Everywhere!	Tackling Social Issues	Sources And Resources, End Notes

Make a plan of action

Keep in mind the following points when making your plan of action:

- Investigate whether or not your local toy stores carry war toys or war video games. If they do sell them, tell the store owners about the campaign and why you feel that it is important. You may be able to convince them to stop selling war toys and war video games. If they do not carry these items, ask them if you can put up a sign about the campaign in the store window. Also, encourage people to buy from these stores to reward the owners for their moral position.
- How will you publicize the campaign?
- Will you need brochures or extra information to educate people about the issue?
- Can you organize an event for the first day of your campaign that will launch the initiative? If so, what will this event consist of? Do you need any guest speakers?
- Will you contact the media? What will be your message? See the section "Working with the Media" beginning on page 82 in Part 3 for helpful hints.

Take action and then review

Take action and have a successful War is Not a Game campaign. Educate people about creating a safer world using the example of war toys and war video games.

Soon after the event, bring your team together and discuss the good points of the campaign, as well as some lessons that the group has learned in order to make a similar event even better next time.

Make sure you thank everyone involved in the campaign.

Have fun!

Have fun while taking part in this worthwhile campaign, and then celebrate your team's success after it is over.

TAKE ACTION! A Guide To Active Citizenship

Home	PART I	PART II
Preface, Contents	How To Get Involved: The Step-By-Step Process	The 'How To' Guide

PART III	PART IV	PART V
Where You Can Get Involved-Everywhere!	**Tackling Social Issues**	**Sources And Resources, End Notes**

Profile: Sadako Sasaki

In 1955, Sadako Sasaki was a young girl with a simple yet heartbreaking dream: she wanted to live.

Born in 1943, Sadako was only two years old when the United States dropped an atomic bomb on Hiroshima, Japan. Many thousands of people lost their lives, yet Sadako survived, and as she grew she blossomed into a happy youth with a love of athletics. She loved to run. One day, however, while training for a big race, Sadako felt ill and nearly fainted. This was unusual for such an outwardly healthy girl.

After testing, doctors confirmed that Sadako had leukemia, the "atom bomb disease." The radiation produced by the nuclear bomb had made her very sick and she was told that she didn't have long to live.

While this was devastating news to Sadako, a friend brought her hope by recalling for her the Japanese legend of the paper crane. It was believed that by constructing 1000 paper cranes, the maker would be granted one wish. For Sadako, it was to be healthy again so she could continue running.

In earnest, Sadako began making cranes with the hope of beating her disease. Sadly, however, she passed away in 1955 at the age of twelve after having folded over 1,000 origami cranes.

It is a sad story, but Sadako's courage, hope, and tenacity inspired her classmates and friends to celebrate her life. They gathered the letters she had written during her illness to form a book and then raised money to build a monument commemorating the thousands of children who lost their lives when the Hiroshima atom bomb exploded.

Today, the monument they built, sitting at Hiroshima's Peace Memorial, is a statue of Sadako holding a paper crane in her outstretched hands.

The base of the statue reads:

This is our cry.
This is our prayer.
Peace in the world.

Sadako Sasaki has inspired many people to dedicate their lives to working for peace. Even now, many years after her death, she continues to do so. Every year, people from around the world send thousands of paper cranes to be placed at the base of her statue to honor peace and to remember Sadako's struggle for life.

MORE ISSUES FOR SOCIAL ACTION

Choose an issue that moves you, do your research, and get involved. What follows are several ideas that might inspire you.

Help to Free Political Prisoners

Write letters to world leaders asking them to free political prisoners. There are thousands of people around the world who have been jailed because they believe in democracy and freedom of speech. You can contact Amnesty International through their website in order to obtain more information about writing letters to help free political prisoners. You can also refer to the section "Writing Letters" beginning on page 39 in Part 3 of this book.

Help Homeless People

Volunteer at a soup kitchen or a local food bank. You can also make a care kit for a homeless person that includes food, a sleeping bag, and some warm clothes. You may want to join a community group to help find long-term solutions for ending homelessness.

Organize a Buy Nothing Day

The world is becoming increasingly materialistic. Particularly in North America, people are encouraged to buy more and more consumer goods. Individuals sometimes tend to forget that happiness is not defined by how many material possessions one owns. A really good way of reminding people of this fact is to organize a Buy Nothing Day. Have your classmates, friends, and family buy nothing for one day to help them realize that there are many more important things in life than possessions.

Educate Youth About Drugs and Alcohol

Educate your classmates and friends about the dangers of drugs and alcohol. Conduct research to find statistics and to learn about the effects of drugs and alcohol. You can give a presentation in front of your class. Starting an after-school club that provides drug-free activities is another great possibility.

Diversity

Our world is filled with so many wonderfully different cultures and languages. Such diversity gives us the continuous opportunity to learn and make new discoveries. Many people, however, look at differences in terms of negatives, which often results in racial conflict. You can encourage people to appreciate differences and to promote tolerance. Start a diversity club at your school. Organize an assembly that highlights different cultural performances. Talk to your school board about including a broader range of ideas and values in your school's curriculum.

Sweatshops

Sweatshops are places where workers are forced to work long hours in inhumane conditions for very little pay. Usually the people who work in sweatshops are women or children. Become informed about the conditions that sweatshop workers endure.

Initiate or join campaigns organized in response to these conditions, and take action to support the struggle of sweatshop workers for better conditions and wages. You are not powerless to help. Start in your own school. Find out if any school materials are manufactured using sweatshop labor by requesting source information on where your school buys its products. Gather a group of supporters and pressure your school board to buy only from manufacturers that provide their employees with just working conditions and do not employ children. You can do this by demanding that companies provide you with a code of ethics, which you can review.

TAKE ACTION!   A Guide To Active Citizenship

PART III	PART IV	PART V
Where You Can Get Involved-Everywhere!	Tackling Social Issues	Sources And Resources, End Notes

There are many organizations you will find to be valuable as you explore issues that are important to you. The following list is only a brief starting point.

HUMAN RIGHTS

Rights and Democracy
1001 de Maisonneuve Blvd. East, Suite 1100
Montréal, PQ
Canada H2L 4P9
Website: www.dd-rd.ca

Human Rights Internet (HRI)
One Nicholas Street
Suite 301
Ottawa, ON
Canada K1N 7B7
Website: www.hri.ca

Human Rights Watch
350 Fifth Avenue, 34th floor
New York, NY
10118-3299 USA
Website: www.hrw.org

Amnesty International USA
5 Penn Plaza, 14th floor
New York, NY
10001 USA
Website: www.amnestyusa.org

Office of the United Nations High Commissioner for Human Rights
UNOG-OHCHR
1211 Geneva 10, Switzerland
Website: www.ohchr.org

TAKE ACTION! A Guide To Active Citizenship

HOME	PART I	PART II
Preface, Contents	How To Get Involved: The Step-By-Step Process	The 'How To' Guide

CHILDREN'S RIGHTS

Free The Children
233 Carlton Street
Toronto, ON
Canada M5A 2L2
Website: www.freethechildren.com

Right to Play
65 Queen Street West
Thomson Building, Suite 1900, Box 64
Toronto, ON
Canada M5H 2M5
Website: www.righttoplay.com

Child Rights Information Network (CRIN)
1 St John's Lane,
London, England
United Kingdom EC1M 4AR
Website: www.crin.org

Children's Defense Fund
25 E Street N.W.
Washington, DC
20001 USA
Website: www.childrensdefense.org

UNICEF
UNICEF House
3 United Nations Plaza
New York, NY
10017 USA
Website: www.unicef.org

ENVIRONMENT

Canadian Parks and Wilderness Society (CPAWS)
National Office
250 City Centre Ave., Suite 506
Ottawa, ON
Canada K1R 6K7
Website: www.cpaws.org

David Suzuki Foundation
Suite 219, 2211 West 4th Avenue
Vancouver, BC
Canada V6K 4S2
Website: www.davidsuzuki.org

Sierra Club
National Headquarters
85 Second Street, 2nd Floor
San Francisco, CA
94105 USA
Website: www.sierraclub.org

National Environmental Trust
1200 18th St. NW, 5th Floor
Washington, DC
20036 USA
Website: www.net.org

United Nations Environment Programme (UNEP)
United Nations Avenue, Gigiri
PO Box 30552, 00100
Nairobi, Kenya
Website: www.unep.org

HUNGER

Canadian Association of Food Banks
2968 Dundas Street West, Suite 303
Toronto, ON
Canada M6P 1Y8
Website: www.cafb-acba.ca

Oxfam Canada
250 City Centre Avenue
Suite 400
Ottawa, ON
Canada K1R 6K7
Website: www.oxfam.ca

RESULTS
440 First Street, NW, Suite 450
Washington, DC
20001 USA
Website: www.results.org

Freedom from Hunger
1644 DaVinci Court
Davis, CA
95616 USA
Website: www.freedomfromhunger.org

Food and Agriculture Organization of the United Nations (FAO)
Viale delle Terme di Caracalla
00100 Rome, Italy
Website: www.fao.org

PART III
Where You Can Get Involved-
Everywhere!

PART IV
Tackling Social Issues

PART V
Sources And Resources,
End Notes

POVERTY

Campaign Against Child Poverty
355 Church Street
Toronto, ON
Canada M5B 1Z8
Website: www.childpoverty.com

Canadian International Development Agency (CIDA)
200 Promenade du Portage
Gatineau, PQ
Canada K1A 0G4
Website: www.acdi-cida.gc.ca

National Center for Children in Poverty
Mailman School of Public Health Columbia University
215 W. 125th Street, 3rd Floor
New York, NY
10027 USA
Website: www.nccp.org

United States Agency for International Development (USAID)
US Agency for International Development Information Center
Ronald Reagan Building
Washington, DC
20523-1000 USA
Website: www.usaid.gov

United Nations Development Programme (UNDP)
One United Nations Plaza
New York, NY
10017 USA
Website: www.undp.org

TAKE ACTION! A Guide To Active Citizenship

| **Home** Preface, Contents | **PART I** How To Get Involved: The Step-By-Step Process | **PART II** The 'How To' Guide |

HIV/AIDS

The Stephen Lewis Foundation
260 Spadina Avenue, Suite 501
Toronto, ON
Canada M5T 2E4
Website: www.stephenlewisfoundation.org

Canadian HIV/AIDS Information Centre
400-1565 Carling Avenue
Ottawa, ON
Canada K1Z 8R1
Website: www.aidssida.cpha.ca

The Body
Body Health Resources Corporation
250 West 57th Street
New York, NY
10107 USA
Website: www.thebody.com

National Aids Fund
729 15th Street, N.W., 9th Floor
Washington, DC
20005-1511 USA
Website: www.aidsfund.org

Joint United Nations Programme on HIV/AIDS (UNAIDS)
Avenue Appia 20
1211 Geneva 27
Switzerland
Website: www.unaids.org

PEACE

Canadian Peacebuilding Coordinating Committee
1 Nicholas Street, #1216
Ottawa, ON
Canada K1N 7B7
Website: www.peacebuild.ca

Foreign Affairs Canada
Enquiries Service (SXCI)
125 Sussex Drive
Ottawa, ON
Canada K1A 0G2
Website: www.fac-aec.gc.ca

Center for Defense Information (CDI)
1779 Massachusetts Avenue NW
Washington, DC
20036-2109 USA
Website: www.cdi.org

Nuclear Age Peace Foundation
1187 Coast Village Road, Suite 1, PMB 121
Santa Barbara, CA
93108-2794 USA
Website: www.wagingpeace.org

United Nations Peace and Security
UN Headquarters
First Avenue at 46th Street
New York, NY
10017 USA

TAKE ACTION! A Guide To Active Citizenship

| **Home** Preface, Contents | **PART I** How To Get Involved: The Step-By-Step Process | **PART II** The 'How To' Guide |

FREE THE CHILDREN

"children helping children through education"

Founded in 1995, Free The Children is the world's largest network of children helping children through education. Through the organization's youth-driven approach, more than one million young people have been involved in innovative programs in more than 45 countries. For its proven track record of success, Free The Children has been widely recognized, including the World's Children's Prize for the Rights of the Child, also known as the Children's Nobel Prize, and established partnerships that include Oprah's Angel Network.

- Provides 50,000 children in the developing world with education daily.
- Has built over 500 schools to date throughout the developing world.
- Delivers school and health kits, 207,500 to date, to students around the world.
- Ships essential medical supplies, $15 million US worth to date, to people in 40 countries.
- Establishes health care projects and centers, helping 505,000 people.
- Implements alternative income projects overseas for poverty-stricken women and their families, helping 23,500 people.
- Provides access to clean water and proper sanitation, helping 138,500 people.
- Supports and assists over a thousand Youth in Action groups throughout North America and across the world.

Visit www.freethechildren.com to find out more.

ME TO WE

Me to We is about living socially conscious and empathetic lives, engaging in daily acts of kindness and building meaningful relationships with others. Living Me to We means committing one's self to always considering the benefits for *we* in our actions, from small choices to major life decisions. On a global scale, it means recognizing our ability to have a positive impact on our planet and in the lives of those around the world most in need.

Me to We is a new kind of social enterprise for people of all ages, offering socially conscious, ethically-minded alternatives to their usual daily choices. Through our media, products and leadership experiences, we directly support Free The Children's work of empowering youth to create global change. Every trip, T-shirt, song, book, speech, thought and smile adds up to a lifestyle that's part of the worldwide movement of *we*.

Together, we can create a worldwide community of 'we thinking' and 'we acting,' where socially conscious choices are the norm and helping our global community drives the simple decisions we make each day.

Visit metowe.com for all the latest updates.

TAKE ACTION! A Guide To Active Citizenship

HOME	PART I	PART II
Preface, Contents	How To Get Involved: The Step-By-Step Process	The 'How To' Guide

ACKNOWLEDGEMENTS

In true Free The Children spirit, this book represents the collective efforts of an extraordinary team of individuals we are honoured to call friends. Our gratitude to Deepa Shankaran and Laoghan Hendra for their dedication to the Take Action! series and their inexhaustible patience throughout the writing process. A huge thank you also to Marisa Antonello and the team at TurnStyle Imaging for their creativity.

A special thank you to Eva and Yoel Haller for their love, Michelle Douglas for her conviction; Dr. Dorothea Gaither for her insight and Dr. John Gaither for his thousands of hours spent volunteering. My appreciation to Rene Malo and his family, along with Clark Peterson and Jonathan Vanger for their dedication to sharing our story.

This book represents the experiences of Free The Children's more than fourteen years of work in the field of human rights and youth empowerment. We are especially grateful for the support of our board of directors, including Chris Besse, Mary Eileen Donovan, Charlotte Empey, Ed Gillis, Gregory Harmandayan, Adrian Horwood, Stephanie Kay, Kathy Sarafian, David Sersta, Lara Steinhouse, Jordana Weiss, Andrew Black, Juliet Bryan-Brown, David Cohen, Josh Cohen, Amy Eldon Turteltaub, Craig Heimark, Libby Heimark, Mary Lewis, Jessica Mayberry, Beverly Cooper Neufeld, Richard Prins, Ernan Roman, Hal Schwartz, Megan Sidhu, Dick Simon, Neil Taylor, Prof. Jonathan White, Monica Yunus, Heidi Hopper and Jim Balle.

And a special tribute to Virginia Benderly and Joe Opatowski, our friends whom we all miss dearly.

Our gratitude goes out to all the organizations and individuals who believe in Free The Children's mission. We would like to extend special thanks to Oprah Winfrey and Katy Davis from Harpo along with Caren Yanis, Tim Bennett, Annie Streer, Christina Timmins and Susan Thome from the Angel Network. We are thankful for the encouragement and support of Leonard Kurz and the Kurz Family Foundation; Julie Toskan-Casale and Diane Elliot from the Toskan Casale Foundation; Linda Rosier, Joe Catalano and the Colours of Freedom team; the Howie Stillman Young Leadership Fund; ONE X ONE; the Solo Family Foundation; the Boyd Foundation; the Journey Foundation; the Sanam Vaziri Quraishi Foundation; the Walter & Duncan Gordon Foundation; the Shapanski Family Foundation; The National Speakers Bureau; Michelle Lemmons and The International Speakers Bureau; the J.W. McConnell Family Foundation; Gerry Connelly, Chris Spence, Allan Hux, Mark Lowry and the Toronto District School Board students, principals and teachers; Taylor Gunn; Charlie Coffee; Bob French; Clive Metz; the Apostolopoulos family; the Joyal family; the Weiss Family; the Heimark family; the Rubin family; and Bob Lato and the Toronto Catholic District School Board.

PART III Where You Can Get Involved- Everywhere!	**PART IV** Tackling Social Issues	**PART V** Sources And Resources, End Notes

We are privileged to count as friends Susan Antonacci and our friends at *Canadian Living*; Martin Regg Cohn and everyone at the *Toronto Star*; Odette and Cristelle Basmaji; Salim Khoja from PowerWithin; Kim Mathewes from Klear Communications; Pi Media Partners; the i2 Foundation; the Skoll Foundation; the Singh Foundation; Buzz Hargrove and the Canadian Auto Workers Union; David Krieger and the Nuclear Age Peace Foundation; dozens of remarkable educators including Greg Rogers, Mary-Eileen Donovan, Mark Fenwick, Nancy DiGregorio and Chris Spence; Karla Wilson and the School Voyageurs team; Larry Moore and the Ontario Library Association team; Lorraine Frost, Ron Common, Dennis Mock and the educators at Nipissing University; Veronica Atkins, Abby Bloch, Jacqueline Eberstein and the Robert C. and Veronica Atkins Foundation; and the entire team at CHUM Limited.

Much appreciation to our corporate and organizational partners, especially the team at National Bank Financial Group, Investors Group, Telus, the Baby Girl Project, Filmplan International II; FreeLife International, Friends of Iqbal; Gibson Foundation; Crofton House School; Sullivan Entertainment; DDB/Rapp Collins; Love Quotes; Lloyd A. Fry Foundation; Sudbury Minga for Maasai; Universal McCann; World Medical Relief; Nokia and Royal St. George's College.

Thank you to Marion Stewart, Joseph Koch, Jane Goodall, David Baum, Glen Kishi, Karen Radford, Jennifer Clarkson, Mark Caswell, Joan Brehl, Tim Broadhead, Patrick Johnston, Lis Travers, Donna Cansfield, Premier Dalton McGuinty, Rebecca Amyotte, Steve Miller, Sue Allan, Walter Green,

TAKE ACTION! A Guide To Active Citizenship

| **HOME** Preface, Contents | **PART I** How To Get Involved: The Step-By-Step Process | **PART II** The 'How To' Guide |

Chris and Tania Carnegie, Terry Reeves, Judith Cunningham, Kate Dernocoeur, Liz Dowdeswell, Kathy Southern, Kerry Shapansky, Patricia Karen Gagic, Elaine Silver, Kim Phuc, Vito Maltese, Leo Ciccone, Dr. Mark Wise and Janelle McFarlane.

We cannot sufficiently sing the praises of the amazing team of staff and volunteers who are the soul of Free The Children and Me to We. The work of Free The Children and Me to We would not be possible without the dedication of many team members who work tirelessly on its mission. Free The Children is blessed to have the tremendous vision and leadership of Dalal Al-Waheidi, who has become family. Me to We's activities have been built by the unwavering dedication and hard work of Renee Hodginkson. Thank you to the leadership team of Victor Li, Janice Sousa, Erin Blanding, Lloyd Hanoman, Shobha Sharma, Peter Ruhiu, Michelle Hambly, William Qi, Erin Barton, Dan Kuzmicki, Lindsey Coulter, Sapna Goel, Allison Sandmeyer, Ashley Hilkewich, Scott Baker, Robin Wiszowaty, Marianne Woods, Kate Likely, Rann Sharma, Caeli Lynch, Alex Apostol and Louise Kent.

The efforts of our young members deserve special praise. Children and youth remain the heart and soul of Free The Children, and it is their dedication to building a better world that has allowed an after-school group to become the world's largest network of children helping children through education. Thank you to everyone who has decided to use their passion and gifts to make a difference!

Finally, our family deserves a heartfelt thank you, especially our Mimi, who remains our biggest fan. Finally, and most important, we wouldn't be where we are today without the love and support of our parents, Fred and Theresa. Thank you for everything, Mom and Dad!

Credits:

Book Content
©2009 Me To We Books

Book Design
©2009 TurnStyle Imaging Inc.

Book Cover Design
©2009 Free The Children

Sillhouette Illustrations
Dane Wirtzfeld...................iii, 62
Kirsty Pargeter.................. ii, 13
Brandon Laufenberg................2
Laura Neal.............................21
James Benet........................104
Springboard Inc................... 147
TurnStyle Imaging...............210
James Thew................. 213-214

Pattern Illustrations:
Tom Nulens, Milan Richter

Printed in China

(Log Out)

Me to We Books share stories that transform your life and the world around you. Our award-winning and best-selling collection includes exciting non-fiction and biographies, curriculum for teachers and inspiring how-to guides. Me to We Books connects a wide range of readers to the latest thinking, stories, trends and issues in social responsibility. Readers aren't just purchasing a book; they're joining a movement.

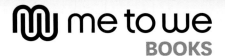

The World Needs Your Kid: How to Raise Children Who Care and Contribute
Craig Kielburger and Marc Kielburger and Shelley Page

This unique guide to parenting is centred on a simple but profound philosophy that will encourage children to become global citizens. Drawing on life lessons from such remarkable individuals as Jane Goodall, Michael Douglas and Archbishop Desmond Tutu, award-winning journalist Shelley Page and Marc and Craig Kielburger demonstrate how small actions make huge differences in the life of a child and can ultimately change the world.

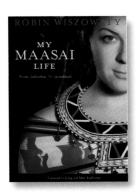

My Maasai Life
Robin Wiszowaty

In her early twenties Robin Wiszowaty left the ordinary world behind to join a traditional Maasai family. In the sweeping vistas and dusty footpaths of rural Kenya, she embraced a way of life unlike she'd ever known. With full-colour photographs from her adventures, Robin's heart-wrenching story will inspire you to question your own definitions of home, happiness and family.

Take More Action
Craig Kielburger and Marc Kielburger and Deepa Shankaran

Written by Craig and Marc Kielburger and Deepa Shankaran, *Take More Action* is an advanced guide to global citizenship, empowering young adults to bring about social change. Brilliantly illustrated and full of powerful quotes, *Take More Action* includes invaluable material on character education, ethical leadership and global citizenship. Ideal for grades 10 and up.

Visit www.metowe.com to order your books today!

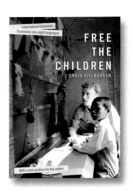

Free the Children
Craig Kielburger

Written by Craig Kielburger on his return from Asia, *Free the Children* is the story that launched a movement. It tells the remarkable story of his encounters with some of the most disadvantaged children on earth, trapped in poverty and exploitative child labour. Winner of the prestigious Christopher Award, it has been translated into eight languages.

It Takes a Child
Craig Kielburger

Illustrated and adapted by Turnstyle Imaging with Craig Kielburger, *It Takes a Child* is a fun, vibrant look back at Craig's adventures in taking global action. Craig takes young readers along on his eye-opening journey throughout the developing world, learning about global issues and making many new friends along the way. Suitable for all ages.

The Making of an Activist
Lekha Singh and Craig and Marc Kielburger

Warning: this book will change you. With vivid images and inspiring words, travelogues, poems and sparkling artwork, *The Making of an Activist* guides you on a journey of positive change, painting an intimate portrait of passionate young activists. Explore the book. Catch the spark.

Visit www.metowe.com to order your books today!